Powers of the Soul

Powers of the Soul

A Kabbalistic Guide To Fulfillment
In This World And The Next

Tom Meyer

LASER PAGES PUBLISHING LTD.

Powers of the Soul by Tom Meyer

© Copyright 2000 by Tom Meyer

Published by: Laser Pages Publishing Ltd.
                     P.O. Box 35409
                     Jerusalem Israel 91352
In cooperation with Upward Bound Books (Israel/U.S.)

Designed and Produced by: Laser Pages Publishing Ltd.
Cover photo: R. Schinlever

ISBN 965-90044-4-3

First edition: March 2000

Printed in Israel by Hemed Press, Jerusalem

Distributed by
Upward Bound Books
tomsher@netvision.net.il

In the United States: In Israel:
P.O. Box 200   26/1 Nachal Refayim
Bergenfield, NJ 07621   Beit Shemesh 97200

Available at bulk order discounts.

To my wife Sheryl

To my mother and father, forever here

Contents

WHAT IS KABBALA AND WHY DO WE NEED IT?

The greatest thing in the world
is to know how to belong to
oneself.
Michel de Montaigne,
Essays, Bk I, 39

JOHN KLUGE IS ONE OF THE RICHEST MEN IN THE world. He has made billions of dollars in the communications industry.

In the spring of 1997 a friend of mine asked Mr. Kluge, "What would you say is your greatest achievement?"

He didn't even hesitate. "Some time ago, I read a newspaper story about a boy in England diagnosed with a terminal brain tumor. The doctors said there was no hope. His parents decided to get him into the Guinness Book of World Records as the person to receive the most Get Well Cards in history. The boy was getting thousands of them in the mail.

"When I read the article in the paper, I sent a telegram saying, 'If you will allow me to do it, I will fly you and your son to the world's greatest brain surgeon, all expenses paid.' Luckily, the parents read it and a short time later I got a phone call from them. I found the greatest brain surgeon — he lived in Pittsburgh — and flew them in. After he finished his diagnosis, he told me that the English doctors were right. The case was hopeless.

"I looked at the brain surgeon and said, 'I have one question. If he were your son, what would you do?'

"He hesitated, then said, 'I'd press for an operation.'

"I told him to do it. And you know what? He healed the boy. That's the greatest accomplishment of my life. I actually saved someone's life."

I love this story.

The answer Mr. Kluge gave should make all of us pause for a moment. He is saying that the most important accomplishment of his life is having saved another human being. He's not saying he doesn't enjoy his money. He *is* pointing out that knowing a good way to use it led to his greatest success.

Nowadays, there are thousands of self-help books. Walk into any bookstore, they seem to explode in your face. Self-help books top the bestseller lists.

These books want us to believe in ourselves. They tell us how to think, how to love and how to become rich.

But there are some very important things they leave out. They don't include the operating manual of what a human being is. Is there such a thing as the soul? If yes, what are its powers?

Nor do they tell us what this universe is all about. Is it chaos and chance? Or is it a vast, brilliant exhibition whose every part contains a message?

They tell us to respect ourselves, but what ultimately brings this feeling and why?

Here is something else the self-help books leave out: we all have different personalities and special talents. How do we discover our unique role in this world? Is there such a thing?

When I was a kid growing up in Detroit, my teachers were a bit embarrassed when I asked these questions. They just shrugged their shoulders and didn't have answers.

Hebrew school didn't help. I went four times a week after regular school, from 4 to 7 p.m. This meant that I missed football and baseball games every day, which really bothered me.

And they weren't answering my questions.

I got my uncle Ruby, the family pediatrician, to help reduce school time.

"The boy needs a lot of fresh air and physical activity," he said to my parents. "Too much school is making him nervous. After all, he's only twelve years old." I kind of tricked my uncle into saying this, but it wasn't hard. He'd disliked school when he was a kid.

It worked. One morning my mother told me I could come straight home from regular school. I didn't have to go to Hebrew school any more. And that was that.

I was free! Baseball, football...and books. I became an avid reader. No one suspected that the skinny kid with the glasses was coming home from the baseball diamond and reading Dickens, Shakespeare and Tolstoy.

This went on through junior high, high school, and then university. I graduated and became a journalist with the Detroit News.

Then I immersed myself in the ancient books of

Judaism, such as the Talmud and Zohar. (We'll talk about these later). I decided never to give a false answer to myself or to a student. I spent ten years in these texts, became a rabbi and taught thousands of classes and seminars all over the world.

This book is the result of what I have learned. It's been a really interesting and fun journey. Now I want to share it with you.

Remove the Blindfolds

Imagine you were put on an airplane and blindfolded. The flight lasts for hours. Finally a gruff voice says, "Okay, get up." A parachute is strapped onto your back, you are taken to a door and pushed out into a blast of wind. You feel yourself hurtling to the earth and, in terror, remember to pull the ripcord. Slowly, you float down until you drop onto a field.

The first thing you do is pull off the blindfold. You see someone walking toward you. When he arrives, what do you think your first question will be?

"Where am I?"

Almost everyone gives this answer.

So why don't people rip their blindfolds off right now and ask, "Where am I?"

The reason is that we get used to the world around us. The streets have names and the houses have numbers, so we think we know where we are.

I once heard about a fellow who had been blind his whole life. One day when he was in his twenties, he woke up and could see. Imagine if that happened to you. You would go outside your house and everything would be stunning! Human machines walking down the sidewalk, birds whirling through the air, huge trees thrust out of the earth, a sky full of deep blue with wisps of white floating across its surface.

What an amazing world.

What is this planet we are on that is hurtling out into space? Why have we been placed into a machine called the "body"? What are all these objects around us? What do they mean?

In order to examine these questions, we need a map — a map of ourselves and of the world around us. Kabbala provides exactly that.

A Brief History of Kabbala

The word "Kabbala" means "receiving" in Hebrew. It refers to the mystical wisdom that was received from the Hebrew prophets and seers of ancient times and handed down to special disciples from generation to generation.

Kabbala explains how the world was created and how it is guided. The details are complicated and vast, but it is well worth the effort to learn the major principles. When one understands Kabbala, he will change forever. Existence will never again be mundane, for he will see how the physical and spiritual are everywhere woven together like the serene luminescence of a sunset.

Kabbala gives great attention to the soul of man, or to be more accurate, the *souls* of man, for each of us has more than one. It describes how an individual can use his spiritual powers to change himself and elevate the world around him. It also focuses on the human physical form, for many details of creation and providence are reflected in it.

It teaches the order of the physical world — the creatures that inhabit it and what they represent. People tend to see only the outer shell.

It explains the direction of individual and world history — both what has happened in the past and what will happen in the future.

And last but not least, Kabbala discusses what happens to the soul after death.

Sometimes Kabbala is alluded to in the Bible, such as in the first chapter of Ezekiel, which was written around 345 BC. But it is described in very obscure terms. This was done on purpose, for much of Kabbala was supposed to remain concealed. Why? It was feared that the ideas would damage the amateur practitioner. Worse, it would give him immense spiritual powers that he might misuse against others.

The information, therefore, was entrusted to the smallest possible circle of masters.

History marched on. Long after Kabbala was given, the Roman army led by Pompey conquered Israel in 63 BC. The Jews, subjected to fierce persecution, revolted over one hundred years later in 69 AD. They were defeated in 70 AD, and their great Temple in Jerusalem was destroyed by fire. All that remained of it was the Western Wall (nowadays sometimes referred to in newspapers as the "Wailing Wall"). Many Jews were enslaved and sent to Rome. The remnant in Israel revolted again in 132. The Romans crushed them three years later.

The Romans decided that the only way to permanently defeat the Jews was to uproot the last traces of their religion. The best method to do this, of course, was to kill all the great sages.

As a result, Kabbala was in danger of being forgotten. To prevent this, it was written down in manuscripts such as the *Sefer HaBahir* (Book of Illuminations), authored by Nechunia ben HaKanah; and the *Pirkei Heichalot* (Book of Chambers).

During this time, a sage named Rabbi Shimon bar Yochai was teaching Kabbala to a group of disciples. He fled from the Romans and was forced to hide in a cave for thirteen years. His teachings, which were not organized in final form for several generations, became known as the *Zohar* (Book of Splendor). The *Zohar* is probably the most influential of all Kabbalistic texts.

The writings of the Kabbalists are incredibly hard to understand. As I said, this was done on purpose. The sages were afraid of putting power in the hands of unworthy students, so they used brief and difficult language to ensure that only someone familiar with the tradition would understand their words.

For centuries, Kabbala was restricted to a very small number of people. In fact, the *Zohar* itself was unknown outside of these students. Only they had the manuscripts. All of this changed when the *Zohar* was finally published in the 1290s. It was like a shot heard around the world, for it immediately gripped people's imagination.

The two greatest Kabbalists of modern times built their intellectual systems based on the *Zohar*. They are Moses Cordovero (1522–1570); and Isaac Luria Ashkenazi (1534–1572), known as the Ari.

The Ari is by far the more widely studied. Only after you understand his writings does the *Zohar* begin to make sense. You can't find any system or structure in it without his help.

The Ari was born in Jerusalem. His father died soon after and his mother moved the family to her brother's estate in Cairo, Egypt.

He began to immerse himself in the study of Kabbala at the age of twenty-one. He would spend weekdays in a house near the Nile, where he prayed and studied completely alone. Then he would return home for the weekend.

He moved to Safed, Israel in 1570 where Moses Cordovero was living. Cordovero died shortly after and the Ari was recognized as the greatest Kabbalist of his generation. He was known as a holy man who could read a person's thoughts and even predict the future.

He left almost no writings of his own. His student, Chaim Vital, wrote voluminous works setting out the teachings of the master. The Ari wanted to instruct only Vital, but the latter invited others to join their sessions. The Ari asked him not to bring them, and warned him that he would regret it, but Vital wanted to share the knowledge with his friends. The Ari's death at a young age was attributed to the revealing of deep secrets to students who were not yet worthy of hearing them.

The Ari died in Safed only two years after his arrival. His tomb there draws many visitors to this day.

The Kabbalists were intensely interested in the soul and personality, which is one of the reasons I am so drawn to them. I have always loved psychology and wanted to understand people better.

The seemingly boundless depth of Kabbala is wonderful. It has helped me learn many of the lessons I am going to share with you in this book.

The Five Souls

According to Kabbala, there are five souls in a human being. They are:

	Hebrew*	*English*
1	Nefesh	Animal Soul
2	Ruach	Spirit
3	Neshama	Upper Soul
4	Chaya	Life Source
5	Yechida	Unique Essence

These five souls form an individual chain, like the links of a necklace which form a single piece of jewelry. One of the goals in life is to unify them so that they are all working together. Then they will connect us back to the Unity of all existence.

Our personalities really consist of the interplay of these souls. Most of the time we are unaware of the upper souls. Yet each one affects us deeply, like the sun shining over a sleeping child.

If we understand each of these souls, we understand ourselves, our drives, what we are meant to accomplish in this world and much of what life is all about.

I have organized *Powers of the Soul* around this framework.

Understanding the first soul teaches us how to interact with our world and get the greatest physical pleasure in a truly positive way.

The second soul teaches us how to be in control of our choices in life and attain a powerful level of self-respect.

---

* In Ruach, Chaya, and Yechida — as in other Hebrew words — "ch" is used to indicate a gutteral consonant as in, for example, the German composer Bach.

The third soul helps us master our mind. This in turn leads us to expanded consciousness.

The fourth soul links us to our purpose in the world. When we understand it, we can write a mission statement for ourselves. This in turn will show us how to establish and meet our life goals. It will also help us improve our personal relationships.

The fifth soul lifts us into a strong bond with the Oneness of the universe — call it God, Unity or whatever word you feel comfortable with. When we come to this section of the book, we'll talk about what happens to the soul after death.

Now let's master ourselves through these five souls and create the lives we want to live.

YOUR BODY AND SOUL

> ...the soul has to be clothed in
> a bodily garment to exist in this
> world.
> *Zohar, Noah, 143*

ACCORDING TO KABBALA, WE ARE A LINK OF FIVE souls placed in the world. Why should we be here at all? Each of us existed before we entered this physical world; we'll exist after we leave it. If so, why do we need to be born?

According to the ancient teachings of Jewish mysticism, our soul knows everything. It knows what each animal is supposed to teach us and how to find God in the leaf of a tree. It knows good and evil and how to raise children. Our knowledge is endless even before birth. But there is one catch — we only know these things *potentially.*

Let me explain. Everyone has seen the movie "The

Wizard of Oz." Do you remember the beginning of the movie? Dorothy and her family are living in Kansas and everything is in black and white. Suddenly, a tornado rips through a field, lifts the house she's in and launches it into the sky. It lands in Oz and from then on the movie is shot in color.

It's the same with the soul. The soul knows everything, but it knows it abstractly, in potential, in black and white. Then, the soul is put into the body and out we pop as a little baby, into a world of color. When the baby is first born, it understands very little. Slowly it begins to accumulate information. Its eyes focus, it sees things more clearly. It begins to respond to sounds, odors, colors and faces. It begins to gain control over its body. It grasps things, it raises its head up. Finally, it can crawl and after a time, stand. Everything is interesting to a baby. We tired adults can barely keep up.

The baby is starting to take the abstract knowledge planted in the soul and turn it into living color.

And when that baby gets older and starts asking questions, my Heavens, watch out! It wants to know everything. Why is the sky blue, why do the leaves drop off in winter, why do dogs bark? There are a lot of ways to answer these questions. Why is the sky blue? We can give an answer from science: it receives its color from sunlight. Sunlight contains all the hues of a rainbow. When it passes through the air, blue scatters the most, giving the sky its color. You can also give a psychological answer — because blue soothes the eyes and relaxes us. So does green, therefore trees are green. Imagine if the sky were red and vegetation purple. Ninety-five percent of humanity would be walking around having a nervous breakdown.

Kabbala teaches us that every object and every color has meaning. Their purpose is to get us to ask questions, discover the wisdom within us and make it real. Then we really have it. It's no longer abstract. For example, every animal teaches us a character trait. Cats teach us cleanliness. When they relieve themselves, they cover it up. Doves teach us chastity — they have one mate their whole life. Ants teach us hard work and humility. Each ant knows its job and does it. Kabbala teaches us that each color conveys a message. Red is justice, white is mercy.

Stay Inspired

When we begin to see the world this way, we suddenly realize that we are in an amazing place. Kabbala warns us that it is very easy to lose the sense of awe that children have. There are four reasons why adults don't pull of their blindfolds and ask, *"Where am I?"*

Desire

The first reason is that they are so busy being distracted by chasing their desires that it never occurs to them to ask. I know I can get like that. If I walk into a wedding and there's great food, I can get so absorbed in eating hors d'oeurves that for a half-hour, I forget to walk up to the bride and groom to say hello. People are out there chasing materialism and the green pieces of paper to pay for it. They can get caught in such a whirlpool that they drown before they get to see the scenery rolling by.

Habit

The second reason people don't ask *"Where am I?"* is that they are used to the world. They just don't notice what's around them anymore. If they saw a hand or an eyeball for the first time, they would be blown away. But they stopped being amazed by anything when they were about three. Maybe if you stuck them in a helicopter and sent them out to Mt. Everest on a really windy day, they would notice something. All of us can get like this.

When I lived in Washington, D.C., and people would ask me if I'd ever been to the Lincoln Memorial or the Washington Monument, I'd say no. They'd look at me incredulously. When it's your city, you just don't go. But when you're on vacation, you want to see everything. After all, you're a visitor. And that's what we are, isn't it? We're visitors. We just get so used to it, we forget to give things a second look. By the way, that's one of the reasons people love going on vacations. They hope to see things in a new way.

Pain

The third reason people don't pull off the blindfold is that they are too focused on the pain, or worse, the bitterness of life. They are so frustrated or mad with something or other, they don't notice anything else.

Meaninglessness

And last but not least, the fourth reason is that we have all been sold a bill of goods. We've been told there is nothing to look for. We've been taught we are just a bunch of dust particles hurtling randomly and meaninglessly through space. Why bother to try to figure it all out — if there is nothing to figure out?

After a quadruple whammy like all of that, is it any wonder that people forget what an amazing world this is?

In order to avoid these pitfalls, we need to understand the first two souls and then harness their powers. To do so, let's now turn to the wisdom of Kabbala.

YOUR FIRST AND SECOND SOULS

> By observing the levels of the soul, you will find the secret of higher Wisdom: and through this Wisdom hidden mysteries will be understood.
> *Zohar, Lech Lecha, 157*

AS I SAID EARLIER, KABBALA TELLS US WE ARE actually not just one soul — we are five.

All five souls are interlocked, like links on a necklace. The healthiest, happiest person has been able to integrate all five units.

We are going to examine all five souls and how they create our identity. Then it will be easier to climb the ladder into being the kind of person we really want to be. By the time we are finished, I promise that you will know a great deal more about yourself and other people.

The Animal Soul

The lowest level of soul is called the *Nefesh* in Hebrew. The word itself actually means "animate" or "enliven." It's often referred to as the *Animal Soul*.

Every species of animal has its own version of this soul. There is a cat Animal Soul, a beaver one and a dog one; moreover, every individual member of the species has its own variation on the theme.

Humans have one, too. The Kabbalists tell us that it rests in the liver and spreads throughout the entire body. It is the soul most affected by what's going on in the body.

How does the body affect it?

If you pick up a pencil, hold it in midair and let go, it will drop to the floor. Why? Gravity, of course.

Gravity is also pulling our bodies down to the earth. This exerts an influence on the Animal Soul. The body itself is a hunk of matter. The Animal Soul is the force of life that animates it. If the Animal Soul departs, the body drops down like a log. We call this death.

There is, of course, a constant gravitational pull on the body. The Animal Soul feels this pull, and turns it into an emotion. It can be laziness — that's fairly common. Imagine carrying around a sack of potatoes all day. You'd get tired pretty quickly. This can happen to us — especially if we are overweight. It can also happen if we are unmotivated. The Animal Soul doesn't know why it has to work so hard and it has this body pulling it down. So it wants to take a nap or lie on the beach.

Another way the Animal Soul can react to gravity is with irritation. Anything impeding the immediate requirements of the body – to sit when it is standing in a long line, to eat when the stomach is growling, to get sex when the body "needs" it — can make the Animal Soul become irritable.

It's easy to see how people get out of control when it comes to food. Their stomach produces chemicals that the Animal Soul becomes aware of and then translates into a message that says, "Eat immediately!" Sometimes the chemicals should be listened to; sometimes the chemicals should be ignored. If you eat every time your stomach rumbles, you are going to bloat up like a whale. If you sleep every time the Animal Soul sends gravity's message to take a snooze, you'll rarely get out of bed. If you have sex every time the Animal Soul picks up a message from the lower half of the body, you might have more children than an amoeba.

Every emotion created by the Animal Soul doesn't have to be obeyed. Sometimes the emotions are good, sometimes they are erroneous. This doesn't mean the Animal Soul is evil or that a physical desire like sex is bad; it only means that the Animal Soul, with all its immense drive and power, has to be taught. Otherwise it will be like a bull in a china shop.

What's so bad about being a bull in a china shop?

It's not just that the bull wreaks havoc on the owner, his shop and all the customers. It also damages *itself.*

When we are out of control and just obeying the Animal Soul, we make life difficult for everyone. We quarrel, we make messes, we hurt our family and our businesses. In the end, we lose our self-respect, too.

Self-respect comes from a person feeling he is good. This is a fundamental, incredibly deep need in all of us. We often try to fulfill it by getting *others* to tell us we are good. How do we do this? We look around our society and notice what people seem to praise: a status job, a big house, a beautiful body. Then we spend the rest of our life chasing it.

True self-respect only comes if we feel we are good. It won't work if others respect our money, our buildings and our bodies — everything but *us*.

How do we get self worth?

In all the times I've gone to funerals, I've never heard a speaker talk about how much money the deceased had in his bank account. No one ever held up a picture of his wife and talked about her hairdos.

They talk about how much money people *gave away.* They talk about the good things the deceased did — he loved his family; she was a caring boss; he helped people.

It's wonderful to have a great house and lots of money, but there are plenty of rich people with low self-esteem. To attain self-respect takes more. We have to feel *we* are good, we have done worthwhile things, we have grown as human beings, we have made a difference in someone's life.

To accomplish this, we can't let the Animal Soul do whatever it wants. Sometimes, as I said, the Animal Soul is right. The body really needs food, sex and clothing.

Other times it is wrong — if, for example, it causes you to steal, manipulate or overeat (in other words, be a bull in a china shop). It may come at you head on like a lion ("go get that piece of cake right now!") or it may sneak up from behind and get you to do things without your realizing that you've been snagged.

The more you blindly listen to the Animal Soul, the weaker you will feel.

Let's talk about how to work with this Animal Soul. What do we do when it hurls demands upon us that are wrong?

The answer seems simple enough: we have to teach it.

In order to teach the Animal Soul what is practical, beautiful and meaningful, we need to answer a question you might have thought of already: Who exactly is the Animal Soul trying to seduce?

The answer is *me*.

Which brings us to the next question: Just who am I?

The Spirit

This question brings us to the second of the five souls that compose a human being. The Kabbalists call it the *Ruach* in Hebrew. In English, it is referred to as the *Spirit*.

Let me repeat that the five souls are all connected like the links of a necklace. The Animal Soul makes demands on the Spirit. It is the Spirit that will decide how to respond. The Spirit is the most fundamental essence of a human being and what distinguishes us from animals. All animals have an Animal Soul. No animal has a Spirit.

The Spirit is the "I" that directs the Animal Soul.

I said earlier that the Animal Soul rests upon the liver. The organ of the Spirit is the heart.

The Spirit contains all good character traits. In a sense, it is perfect. Its only weakness is that it has a blind spot. When the Animal Soul makes a demand, the Spirit can listen to it blindly and do what the Animal Soul wants.

This brings us to an extremely important point: *the Spirit has free will.*

The Animal Soul doesn't have free will — it comes at the Spirit with an impulse. The Animal Soul wants to feel pleasure. It just thinks that grabbing what's in its path will do the job. This is like a baby putting everything in its mouth. Sometimes it tastes good, other times not.

If the Spirit educates it, the Animal Soul will change. It has been taught.

If the Spirit doesn't teach it, the Animal Soul will overcome the Spirit and get it to choose the wrong thing, making everyone miserable in the end.

Since the Spirit is the source of all good traits and it has free will, if the Animal Soul wants the Spirit to choose something, it has to convince it. Think about this. Since the Spirit only wants to do good (it's the source of all good traits), the Animal Soul must therefore come to the Spirit with a rationalization.

This explains a great enigma. Why do human beings justify themselves so much? Just do lousy things and admit it! Why not say, "I stole because I wanted the money?" "I yelled at my wife because I wanted to take my bad day out on someone."

Nope, it never happens this way. "She deserved it." "Society owes me." "He had it coming."

Why do we rationalize? Because the Spirit wants to be good and will never make a choice unless it is convinced it is right. So the Animal Soul has to trick it.

Let me give you an illustration:

Sam has bleeding ulcers. They have made him so ill, he's finally decided to take a day off from work and go to the doctor. After a thorough examination, the doctor looks sternly at Sam and says, "I'm sorry, but I'm going to have to read you the riot act. You have been taking terrible care of your health. I can give you a lot of advice about slowing down on work, watching your diet and taking vacations, but I know you won't listen. There is, however, one piece of advice I absolutely demand you follow: I do not want you to drink orange juice for the next six months. If you do, it'll tear through the lining of your stomach and you'll end up in the hospital. I'm telling you this because I know how much you love orange juice."

"Doctor, I'll do what you say," says Sam. "I'm going to lay off the orange juice."

That evening Sam goes to bed early. He wakes up in the middle of the night and is extremely thirsty. He gets up, goes to the kitchen and turns on the faucet. There's no water! Something happened to the pipes. He's too tired to check it out, he just wants to drink something and go back to bed. So he walks to the refrigerator and opens the door. Lo and behold, the only thing to drink is orange juice.

Now begins the war.

"I can't drink that orange juice," says Sam (the Spirit is speaking here). "The doctor told me how dangerous it is."

"Aw, come on!" says another part of him (the Animal Soul, which has picked up on the body's need for liquid). "What's one lousy drink gonna do?"

"But the doctor said one drink could put me in the hospital" says the Spirit.

"The doctor did say that," agrees the Animal Soul. "But are doctors always right? Doctors make mistakes."

"But how could it be worth the risk?" says the Spirit.

"There is no risk," says the Animal Soul confidently. "First of all, I'm going to go right back to bed and never know the difference. Second, I'm only going to have half a glass. That's sensible and responsible."

Bad advice, Sam. Hold off until daylight and go to a grocery. It's not worth the risk.

This is how the Animal Soul always operates. It has to be educated — by a Spirit determined to make the right choice. The Animal Soul doesn't want to be stupid, it just wants to be comfortable. The Spirit *always* wants to be good. That's why it has to be tricked.

I can tell you right now, people are able to come up with rationalizations for anything. Prisons are full of people convinced they did no wrong.

Types of Anger

Just to make sure that you know how the whole system works, let's take an emotion like anger and watch the interplay between the Animal Soul and the Spirit.

Animal Soul anger

An elderly lady is walking down a hallway in an office building. A man accidentally bumps into her.

Strong emotions sweep into her. These emotions are saying, "How dare he push his way around like that? Does he think he owns the building?" If she loses control, she'll yell at the startled fellow.

If we give into anger like this often enough, it becomes so much a part of the Animal Soul that it turns into a trait. That's the difference between someone who is momentarily angry, and someone who is an *angry person*.

Spirit anger

Let's look at an example where anger can be used properly. Our same elderly lady is walking in the park. She sees three big boys shouting out racial slurs at a little girl who is crying. So our heroine — the same woman — walks over to the boys and rebukes them until they leave the girl alone.

This is actually spiritual anger. Here, the Spirit directs the Animal Soul to be indignant and not watch the scene passively.

\\\\\\\\\\\\\\\\\\\\\\\\\\\\\\\\\\\\

There are two terrible ideas to which we must *never* give in when we deal with the Animal Soul:

1) **The Animal Soul is rotten. All it wants to do is indulge in food and sex.**

   Never hate the Animal Soul. Work with it and teach it.

   You can run away from marriage, good food and living in a nice house, and become a total ascetic. But it means you run away from a lot of the pleasures and meaning in life — things you could have enjoyed in a wonderful way.

   The Animal Soul should never be made to feel it is disgusting. Smother the Animal Soul, and you smother your drive for living. Instead, it should be lifted and joined to the higher levels of the soul.

2) **If it feels good, do it.**

   This is also ridiculous. Every impulse of the Animal Soul isn't holy.

   The Spirit must make good choices. It must teach the Animal Soul to desire beauty and meaning, rather than constant, immediate gratification.

\\\\\\\\\\\\\\\\\\\\\\\\\\\\\\\\\\\\

Now it's time for another question. It takes effort for the Spirit to master the Animal Soul. Why can't we just change all our habits overnight? To this interesting question we will now turn our attention.

THE DEVELOPING CHILD

It is easier to resist at the begin-
ning than at the end.
Leonardo Da Vinci,
The Notebooks, Vol I, Ch. 2

THE ANIMAL SOUL HAS AN OVERWHELMING
advantage in the early portions of our life. This is because
the Spirit never enters the fetus.

At first, this seems to conflict with Kabbalistic sources
that say the fetus knows all wisdom and can "see from
one end of the world to the other." This is true only in the
sense that the Spirit hovers above the fetus, though it is
not drawn into the body itself. Being in a physical home
does not yet constrict it; therefore, it can see everything.
Kabbala says that "A candle is lit above the head of the
baby" to make this point.

At this stage, the Animal Soul has entered the body
and gives it life. It has the playing field all to itself.

After the baby is born, the Spirit begins to enter the body — but the baby doesn't remember the wisdom now located *inside* its physical house. This is a very important idea. It teaches us that in potential, human beings know all truth. They have all good character traits just waiting to be activated, once they have the power to do so.

In the beginning years, of course, the baby has an intense inclination toward immediate gratification. It doesn't discern good and bad yet, for the needs of the body overwhelm the Animal Soul and the Animal Soul in turn overwhelms the Spirit.

As the baby grows — if he or she is educated and taught properly — the powers of the Spirit gain strength and begin to dominate. For this to happen the right way, parents must focus on two things:

1. **Developing the child's intellect**

2. **Developing the child's character**

In other words, the parents must help the child learn how to guide his Animal Soul. By the time the child reaches his teenage years, his Spirit is sufficiently developed to be able to become independent. He can make good decisions on his own.

But what happens if his parents and teachers have not given him clear understanding? What if they have not trained him to recognize the difference between the Animal Soul and his more spiritual components?

They haven't taught him how to choose. He's grown accustomed to listening to his impulses.

Remember, the Spirit has the power to choose. This young person doesn't want to hurt himself or anyone else. He's beautiful inside — but he's trying to ride a wild bronco!

A child is very much affected by the messages of his environment. If the environment around him teaches him how to deal with the Animal Soul, he can become an early master of it. It will be work, because the Animal Soul had the early edge.

But if the environment tells him, "Do whatever feels good" and he listens, not only will the Animal Soul have an early edge — it will get the Spirit to lead its armies. By the time he reaches the teenage years, he ignores his spiritual powers. Get ready for late nights and lots of worrying! And he can give you fifty reasons for everything he does.

Personality is not just molded by environment, however. I said earlier that the Spirit enters the body at birth. We see that every baby has its own character. Different aspects of the Spirit shine through at birth in every one of us. In one baby, it shines through and dominates the Animal Soul in kindness; in another baby, it may be endless curiosity or determination.

Light in the Womb

Imagine the Spirit as a light, and the Animal Soul as a dark cover placed upon it with little portals of glass. Light shines through the portals. The more portals that are open, the more the Spirit shines through. The more portals that are closed, the more the Spirit is blocked.

Every human being has different portals that have been opened at birth. His job is to open more of them. Every right choice opens portals or even creates new ones; every wrong choice closes them.

Often the difficulty in understanding someone's personality comes from the interplay between how the child comes out at birth, and what was shaped by his environment.

At birth, a child might come out gentle. That's the portal that's open naturally. The environment could train the child to be aggressive, which can also be a good trait if expressed properly. The Animal Soul will learn this trait and the child will develop into an aggressive person. Deep underneath, he is gentle, but no one would guess it because the Animal Soul suppressed it and a different portal was opened.

Here is another example: a child can have a natural inclination toward being brave and the environment can brainwash him into being cowardly.

When we meet somebody, it's important to evaluate what aspects of his personality are the ones he was born with, and which are the ones he has developed. It's not easy, but it's very important — this helps us know something about the root from which his soul descends. (More about this later.) One thing is certain: the bad things are not from the Spirit — they are from an uneducated, or wrongly educated Animal Soul.

Maturity

The Kabbala teaches that by the age of thirteen, the Spirit has fully entered the body. Potentially, teenagers have total power over their decision-making abilities. They have free will. That's why they begin to exert their independence so much.

This is a great time to discuss free will more deeply. What exactly is it and how do we use it efficiently? This is the subject of the next chapter.

5   MAKING GREAT CHOICES

> Never consider anything to be
> an advantage to you that will
> make you … lose your self-re-
> spect.
>
> *Marcus Aurelius Antoninus,*
> *Meditations, III, 7*

WE USE OUR FREE WILL LOTS OF TIMES EVERY DAY,
often without being aware of it. We really need to be sure
that we are making the choices that count.

Let's make it clear at the outset that I am not talking
about the choice between eating vanilla or chocolate ice
cream. That's not a choice, but a preference. At 2 p.m., I
may have a desire for chocolate, at 7 p.m., for vanilla.

Animals exhibit preferences, too. If you put a hamburger and a bone in front of a dog, the dog will pick one
or the other. This is an urge, a mood, and not what I mean
by free will.

Some people think free will is about the choice between
good and evil. There are several reasons why looking at it

this way is not productive. First, it leads to college dormitory-style arguments about the nature of good and evil. Some people will say "x" is good, other people "y". Then there are the folks who say there's no such thing as good and evil.

The truth is, people always *think* they are choosing "good." The most vicious murderer in prison will tell you why he was doing the right thing. He will have a justification. Believe me, I have talked to them. They all have a list of rationalizations for what they did.

Choose Life

Free will is not about preferences, or good and evil. *It is about choosing life rather than death.*

The Bible puts it in an interesting way in Deuteronomy 30.19:

> *"I have set before you life and death, the blessing and the curse; choose life, that you may live."*

You may be startled by what I am saying. After all, who would choose death? My answer is: sometimes all of us do.

What do I mean?

As I have said, our physical bodies are chunks of matter. Gravity pulls matter downward. The Animal Soul detects the pull of gravity on the body and converts it into an emotion. That emotion is the desire to sleep, to avoid pain, to escape effort, to give up. Psychologists call this "the death wish."

On the lowest level, there are people who simply commit suicide. I've been involved in four situations where someone wanted to commit suicide. Each one gave as the explanation, "I have no reason to live, no purpose in going on."

Each of these potential suicides was saying, "It hurts, I want to give up."

The power of choice resides in the Spirit. In order for the Animal Soul to get its way, it must convince the Spirit to choose death. If it wins, the person will commit suicide. For most of us, this doesn't happen. If the Animal Soul comes like this at the Spirit, the Spirit says, "No, silly. Life has a lot of good to it. We're not going to commit suicide."

But gravity hasn't stopped exerting its pull, so the Animal Soul tries a new strategy. "Okay" it says, "we won't commit suicide. Instead, let's stay in bed half the day." This message comes to the Spirit. Some people go with it – they choose a new form of death. I've met such people. Try to get them to do anything. They are depressed, unmotivated. They sleep long hours. That's because their Spirit has not taught their Animal Soul that life is worth living.

They have focused on choosing death. If the Spirit wins this battle, and it does for almost all of us, the Animal Soul will try yet another diversion. "You want to get out of bed? Fine. Then let's watch television all day."

This is a good one. Sometimes television is valuable — it can teach us things or relax us after a stressful day. But let's not forget that it's mostly passive. A couch potato sits, his eyes staring ahead, his mind flat, and he absorbs. He doesn't have to do anything. He's only making one choice — to keep his eyes open.

For the most part, that is not much of a choice. A little bit of TV can be good. But a large daily dose is the choice of a waking sleep — in other words, a subtle form of death.

But let's say the Spirit says, "No! I want to grow! I want to do something meaningful in life." The Animal Soul usually says, "Good, let's get some ambition, some direction — let's get a career!" A person might get a career either because he needs money to survive, or he is looking for some kind of meaning. Bed and television just aren't enough. Having a career does add meaning to life. Something is being built. It is a form of choosing life, of helping oneself and hopefully others. It's necessary and truly worthwhile.

But a job can ultimately become a form of escape, too. It can become a rut. I have seen people immerse themselves in their jobs so thoroughly that they neglected their family and themselves. Even someone fortunate enough to have a job that is extra-meaningful may lose sight of the fact that there are other important facets of life.

Usually at some point in a person's career, a gnawing doubt works its way into his heart. *"There must be more to life than this."* This comes from the drive of the Spirit for meaning and purpose.

The Animal Soul is always seeking comfort and it has found it in the form of a job. Sure, work is hard with lots of long hours, but at least the person can ignore life's ultimate questions. But the doubts begin to pressure him.

So he begins to experience a great inward struggle. Some people think this usually happens in middle age (the so-called mid-life crisis). I've actually seen it in teenagers and up. And I've seen it in very successful people, as well as folks with hardly a nickel in their pocket.

If the Spirit wins, the person will start to look in additional directions: family, a cause, spirituality. If he chooses one of these, he begins a new journey.

The hourglass of life always moves. Either we put down our bags and call it quits somewhere along the way, or we keep going forward.

The trick is not to focus on the difficult moments, but the fabulous gains involved as we build friendships and families, as we grow in spirituality, as we look at the world around us and all of its beauty. We can have spiritual experiences and feel ourselves part of an awesome Oneness. I have often asked people to make a list of their five greatest experiences. No one has ever listed sleeping an extra four hours or watching a television program. Rarely do they list their job. The list usually includes things like a trip to the mountains, the birth of a baby, being married to someone they love and who loves them, a moment of deep spiritual insight, or helping other people (like the story of John Kluge at the beginning of this book).

In other words, a moment where they experienced life, not death.

Perhaps I have made this sound like a lot of effort. Sometimes it is, but it's immensely pleasurable and a great deal of fun — if we do not see the Animal Soul as an enemy, but as a friend or a child that we enjoy teaching.

By the way, people often ask me a great question: If I'm saying the Animal Soul causes so many problems, why aren't *real* animals totally messed up? If the Animal Soul wants sleep, comfort, and at its craziest moment even suicide, why aren't real animals jumping off ten-story buildings?

The answer is, animals are programmed differently. It's not that they have a Spirit telling them to seek meaning and not jump off a building — animals don't *have* a Spirit. They only have an Animal Soul. But, whereas the human Animal Soul has to be trained to seek what is good for it, animals are already programmed that way. Their Animal Soul instinctively seeks what works for it.

We humans are created with an Animal Soul that needs to be taught and a Spirit capable of teaching it. This ultimately gives us our sense of accomplishment and self-respect. We are more than robots. We may sometimes make wrong choices, but at least they are ours. And we can make great choices, too.

Focus on the Goal

It sometimes seems difficult to master the Animal Soul and teach it to want things that are really good for it.

In truth, it is not so hard. I am going to show you a technique that will actually make it easy to use your free will in a positive way and move toward true greatness.

Let me start by giving you an example. Let's say we are standing at one end of a giant room. I ask you to run to the other end.

You look at me a bit puzzled. "Why should I do that?" you ask.

I say, "Just trust me."

"OK," you say, and off you go to the other end.

When you get there, I call out, "Hey, run back here now." You run back a little slower. As you arrive, I bark out, "Go to the other end again."

Most people won't do it. They'll say, "I'm not going to just run back and forth without a reason."

A few folks, the ones who are usually the teacher's pets, will race off to the other end again. Sooner or later, at most after four or five trips, my track team is going to dissolve to zero.

But what if I put baskets up at each end of the room and hand out a ball? Did you ever watch a basketball game? People are running around so much, it can make your head spin. What's different?

I'll tell you what's different: they have a goal, a purpose. If I stick a scoreboard on the wall, 20,000 cheering fans into the stands and pay the players $10,000 a game, they'll run with aching heels, bodies dripping with sweat, elbows flying, and be ready to break my neck if I threaten to take them out of the lineup.

The minute the Spirit knows what it wants, the Animal Soul will follow along happily. Clear goals with a powerful motivation always win.

The Animal Soul wants to be motivated. It wants to be led by the Spirit. But if it isn't, it focuses on the pain and effort and just wants to give up and rest. With clear goals, it hardly notices the sweat. If I pay an adult $1000 an hour to play hopscotch, he'll do it all day until he has so much money that he's not motivated by it anymore. But if I don't give him anything, he will be worn out after a minute and a half.

Motivation comes from seeing the goal. It can be related to money, love, happiness, respect and a lot of other things.

Empower the Spirit

The only way of giving the Spirit power to educate the Animal Soul and lift it into beauty and meaning, is by knowing how to use free will effectively. Remember – free will resides in the Spirit. The Animal Soul does not have free will. It tries to manipulate the Spirit, but if the Spirit deflects the seductions of the Animal Soul it will be in the driver's seat.

There are five critical steps in training the Spirit to be totally in charge of the Animal Soul:*

Step 1. Be aware of the choices you are making.

We often don't realize what we are doing. The other day, I met a couple considering divorce. They were both nice people, but very different. The man was an investment broker – logical, practical and critical. The woman was an actress. She grew up in a show-business family that never created rules or any kind of framework for her. She always went by feelings, which were sometimes pretty subjective.

If they had known how to respect each other and work together as a team, he could have given her some of his skills. She could have taught him how to loosen up, have fun and enjoy the pleasures of life. But they did not know how to communicate.

She wanted to get pregnant. He would hear nothing of it until their marriage was sorted out.

After meeting with them for an hour over dinner, I saw the choices they were making. He was going to go on disapproving of her until she would get fed up and walk out on him. She was going to stay in the relationship until she was so miserable, she would have to flee. Neither one knew how to either create a healthy partnership or end it gracefully.

So they were choosing to let events run their course until the marriage sank from the weight of its own misery.

---

*My ideas about these steps in mastering free will were greatly influenced by Rabbi Noah Weinberg, Dean of Aish HaTorah Rabbinical College in Jerusalem. He is, among many things, quite a genius at definitions.

That was their choice. They were seeing marriage counselors and psychiatrists, but no one was able to help them because they were unwilling to change their behavior. They were only prepared to choose to float.

I pointed this out to them. It had no effect. Then I said to them, "Listen, why don't you write a new marriage contract? Write down what you're willing to commit to. When the contract is finished, call me up. If you don't do it, I'm not going to meet with you again."

I was trying to get them to be aware of the choices they were making.

A week later, they faxed me the contract. It was actually quite good. They promised to work at seeing the positive in each other. "Any criticism of the other person," they wrote, "will be meant to help and not to hurt, and will be given gently and sparingly." They also agreed to spend one evening together every week, doing something they both enjoy.

Their outlook has changed. They're now more aware of what they're doing. And their marriage is working.

Choices, of course, don't have to be caused by crises. People decide they are at a point in life where they are ready to get married or change careers. They decide to take a special vacation with their kids to get closer to them. They do it not because they are forced to, but because they are *happy* to. The point is to be aware of our choices.

Step 2. Understand the assumptions behind your choices.

Let me illustrate what I mean. Every person lives in an intellectual "house" he has constructed. Every brick in it is an idea that has been mortared in place. It can be something he thought out himself, read in a book or heard as a kid. I am not saying it is *wrong* to build a house of ideas. We have to do it — it gives us our way of looking at the world. We just have to make sure it is built with the right materials. A faulty brick weakens the wall. A faulty foundation is even more dangerous and can cause the whole building to collapse.

Let's look at the assumptions behind some of the choices people make.

I was once with a cabdriver who gave me seven reasons why he wasn't going to open up his own business. It wasn't the right time, the economy was going down, he didn't have enough capital, he'd be away from his kids too much, etc.

When I questioned him, I soon uncovered the true assumption that was making him afraid. He actually said it himself: "You know what? It's just too late. Life has passed me by."

"How old are you?"

"Thirty-five."

Thirty-five years old and it was too late for him? Colonel Sanders started to build Kentucky Fried Chicken when he was in his sixties!

If we don't think through the assumptions behind our choices, we become puppets of society, or of our own bad information, or of decisions we made that no longer apply (and may have been silly to begin with). When you choose something be sure to ask yourself, "Why am I doing this? What's the assumption behind it?"

I knew a woman in her mid-eighties whose son lived in another state. He wanted her to leave her apartment and move in with him. She was getting too old to live alone.

She gave good reasons for not leaving. She trusted her doctors, the weather suited her more where she was and she liked the people in her building.

He fought with her on each issue. One day, it finally occurred to him that she was staying put because she didn't think her son's wife really wanted her. Even the mother didn't consciously realize the reason for her decision.

When the son understood this, he asked his wife to phone her. After that the mother decided to move. Her choice went from, "I won't move, I don't think I'm wanted" to "I am wanted. I am ready to go." Her assumption had been wrong in the first place.

For the couple who I asked to write out a marriage contract, the husband's assumption was "My wife will never act consistently." The wife's assumption was, "If he truly cared about me, he would accept me no matter what I do."

And why did she think he should accept her no matter what she did? Her way of looking at marriage was that a spouse should go along with the other person's choices. But it wasn't working. He didn't want a marriage partner whose behavior was throwing his life into turmoil.

These kinds of examples happen all the time. That's why it's important to understand the assumptions behind our choices.

Step 3. Recognize the conflict between what the Spirit wants and what the Animal Soul feels like doing.

The Spirit wants meaning, beauty, love. The Animal Soul desires sleep, comfort and immediate gratification.

The old woman *wanted* to live with her son, but she *felt* like avoiding the possibility of rejection.

The cab driver *wanted* to start a business, but his Animal Soul was afraid of the pain of failure. The Spirit could have taught the Animal Soul that failure does not mean "you stink," or that you're finished for life. You can learn from mistakes and improve.

The unhappy couple — their Spirits *wanted* to learn how to communicate and share with the other person. Their Animal Souls *felt* that the other person would never change, so it was easier to quit. That was the inner conflict each of them was experiencing.

Step 4. Identify with your Spirit, not your Animal Soul.

We all know we shouldn't invest money according to any impulse that comes into our head. Sure, we'd win a few — but in the end, we'd all go broke.

The same is true about all other impulses. Check them out and see if they are destructive. You can be spontaneous, but before you take a running dive into the cement pool make sure there's water in it.

When a feeling rampages at me to eat that extra piece of seven-layer chocolate cake, I remind myself that it's the body talking through the Animal Soul and it may not be right.

The cabdriver who was afraid to start his own business — wouldn't he sound funny if he said, "My Animal Soul feels like giving up, but I'm going to teach it otherwise!" Of course he would. But that's only because he's used to thinking that all his impulses are the real him.

Remember — the Animal Soul isn't evil or satanic. It just needs to be straightened out a bit, as you would educate a child you love. And don't get down on yourself if you have a hard time doing it. No one is perfect, and every mistake is a chance to learn something new.

Impulses and emotions are felt in the heart. Kabbala teaches us that the Animal Soul rests on the liver and makes itself felt through the left part of the heart, and the Spirit through the right side.

I wouldn't recommend having a friend stick his head against your chest the next time you have an emotion, the way cowboys in the movies put their heads to the ground to figure out the direction of approaching horses.

But it is a good idea to ask yourself who is speaking, the Animal Soul or the Spirit. Then identify with the Spirit. Say things like, "I don't need that second hamburger right now."

However, if you do — eat it!

And if you get a Spirit inspiration, try to go with it. For example, let's say you're in a glum mood one morning. You didn't get a good night's sleep, you're late for work and the toast came out burned. You walk outside and find yourself gaping at a beautiful spring day. Give yourself a second to enjoy it. You'll feel a shot of pleasure course through your whole body from the sheer wonder of being alive. That terrific emotion energizes you because there's no conflict between the Animal Soul and Spirit — you've taken charge and both of the souls have been lifted into beauty.

Your Animal Soul is good, too. It just needs to be led in the right direction.

Step 5. Choose life.

Remember what we said earlier: free will is not a question of choosing good or bad, but choosing life rather than death. We all want life, happiness and meaning. But floating through life or obeying the Animal Soul won't get you there.

Choosing well and following through with your decisions takes effort. That's the price we pay for becoming great human beings. I once asked Yitzchak Perlman, the world-famous violinist, how he learned to play so wonderfully.

"I worked hard at it my whole life," he said.

I didn't sense someone who felt he had lost anything by the effort. If anything, I admired his love of the craft and humility toward the music he has mastered.

Some people avoid choices (which in itself is a choice) because they are afraid of the pain of failure. The truth is, they fail by not trying. After I first finished university, I became a journalist for the Detroit News. I had a close friend who had a lot of talent as a writer and I urged her to come for a tryout at the newspaper. She kept putting it off.

One evening I went to her house. "Judy," I said (I've changed her name), "everything is set up for two days from now. I'm going to pick you up and take you to the office. A friend of mine is going to test you. It will be totally painless. Even if you don't do well – which I know won't happen – I'll coach you for the next tryout until you pass with flying colors and get a job there."

"Absolutely not!" she said. "It's just not the right time."

"But you've been saying that for weeks. I know you desperately need the money. You're just hanging around and eating through your savings."

"No way," she repeated. "I'll be busy all week."

I finally realized what was going on. I could see it in her eyes. She was afraid of failing, so she avoided trying at all. But that in itself was a form of failure. Why couldn't she just go for the fun of it? She would be choosing life because, even if she didn't pass the test, she would learn from the experience and do better next time.

President Franklin D. Roosevelt once said, "We have nothing to fear but fear itself." There is real wisdom in these words.

This reminds me of the story about the fellow who was driving home from work one day and stopped to watch a Little League baseball game. As he stood behind the bench on the first-base side, he asked one of the boys what the score was.

"We're behind 11 – 0," he answered with a smile.

"Really? I must say, you don't look very discouraged."

"Discouraged?" the boy answered with a puzzled look on his face. "Why should I be discouraged? We haven't been up to bat yet."

That's what I call confidence!

If you use all five steps of free will, your Spirit will be the rider and the Animal Soul its horse.

Self-Respect

When we are afraid to use our free will or we use it destructively, we risk losing our self-respect.

When we identify with our Spirit, we teach and inspire the Animal Soul so that we achieve our goals. Then we'll feel great about ourselves.

I'd like you to do an exercise that people find incredibly valuable, though it sometimes makes them a bit nervous. Have you ever thought about what you would like written on your tombstone? I bet not. I once put the question to a group of prominent businessmen in Washington, D.C., and one of them said, "Somebody else's name." It got a great laugh.

It's a productive exercise, because it shows what is most important to you in life and how you want to be remembered. So here is a drawing of a tombstone. Let's see how you fill it in.

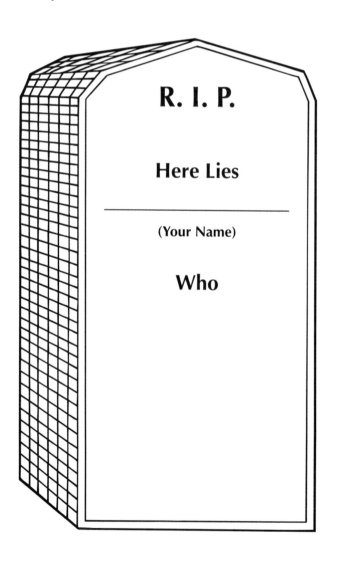

R. I. P.

Here Lies

_____

(Your Name)

Who

What you wrote is a good indicator of how your Spirit wants to use free will. The Spirit is usually speaking here — I never saw somebody write, "Here lies Jack Smith who ate 5000 chickens." Or, "Sam Jones lies here. Boy did he mess up his kids!"

If you want "He was a good father" or "She was a good mother" chiseled in your *real* tombstone, it will mean making important decisions and following through on them. (To "chisel" means "to cut with a chisel." It also means "to trick, to cheat." These seem to be the two choices — you can work at being a good parent or try to fool your kids.)

If you want "He was a good friend" or anything meaningful on your tombstone, you will have put the Spirit in charge so it can properly direct the robust drive of the Animal Soul.

By the way, here is what I wrote on my tombstone when I did this exercise:

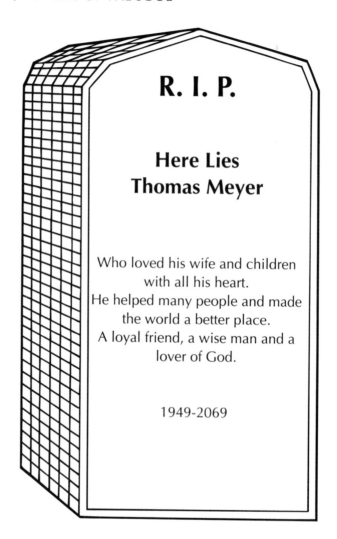

R. I. P.

**Here Lies
Thomas Meyer**

Who loved his wife and children
with all his heart.
He helped many people and made
the world a better place.
A loyal friend, a wise man and a
lover of God.

1949-2069

Let's see, I wrote that I lived from 1949 to 2069. I sure hope I'm still healthy at 120 years of age!

6 FOUR WAYS TO LIVE

> The way a person desires to go, he is led.
>
> *Talmud Bavli,*
> *Makkot, 10b*

NOW THAT WE UNDERSTAND SO MUCH ABOUT free will, let's look at the four ways we pursue goals. Then it will be easy to understand where our choices are leading us.

1. We can abuse the world

2. We can use the world

3. We can take pleasure in its beauty

4. We can look for its meaning

To tap into the powers of the first and second soul, it pays to pick the right strategy. Let's see what impact these four ways of pursuing goals have on the following aspects of our life: houses, food, sex and vacations.

Houses

Abuse

When I talk about abusing a house, I don't mean you don't mow the lawn, you don't repair the roof and all the neighbors hate the fact that you are bringing down property values. That stuff is obvious. So is blasting music out the window so loudly that you keep the neighbors up. But there are other forms of abuse of a house.

One is status. You build a mansion because you want to impress people and show them how great you are. If anyone walked around with a sign that said, "I have 250,000 bricks in my house, which is twice as many as you have," you'd think he was a fatheaded buffoon. Of course no one would be so crass as to state it, but sometimes, this is what's going on.

That's not just abusive to other people, telling them that they are nobody because their house is smaller; it's also abusive to ourselves. Why would anyone work sixteen hours a day and kill himself to have a lot of doors and windows, for the sole purpose of impressing other people? Someone like that neglects his wife, children and friends just to build a personal skyscraper. In their hearts, people know it is ridiculous. I bet you have never been to a funeral where the person giving the eulogy held up a picture of the home of the deceased and said, "You know what was great about Joe? He had one heck of a mansion!"

Use

I've often asked groups of people, "What's the purpose of a house?"

The first thing people say is food, shelter and recreation. This is a practical answer. We want a place to put our beds and books, a place to hang our pictures. We need privacy. And some people really do need a big house to have a feeling of spaciousness.

Beauty

The third level is beauty. This can be very positive. A beautiful house, beautiful furniture and pleasant rooms give people pleasure and help them feel the goodness of life. They literally can't wait to get home! The lawn is beautiful, the architecture is beautiful. This is a very positive thing.

The Talmud* says, "Three things expand the mind: a nice house, nice clothes and a nice marriage."

Meaning

A house is a place that should nurture two things: learning and giving to others.

In terms of learning, the Talmud says: *"Make your home a gathering place for wise people."* This can be done through books and movies that teach something. That's the difference between a house and a home. A house is just a building. A home is a place where we grow together with our spouses and teach values to our children.

Concerning giving to others, the Talmud says we should open our door wide for the poor. This means our home can be a place where we give charity to people who are in need. We create an environment where people want to come in and share; where, for example, kids in the neighborhood feel they can find people they can talk to.

---

*The Talmud is a vast body of wisdom and laws completed by great Rabbinical sages around 500 AD.

Money, time, sympathy and advice are all ways to give.

This doesn't mean you should let dangerous drifters in the door; or that every kid with a problem can bang on your door and get your attention at all hours, to the detriment of time with your own family. Each person must decide what is best for himself, in terms of what he can give.

Time is often more difficult than money. It's easier to write a check than get involved with some kid who's not getting along with his folks. Whatever you decide, your children will learn valuable lessons from watching you.

Some people can do this better in a big house, some in a small one. If your goal is clear and has meaning, then even if you want to live in a big house but cannot afford it, that doesn't make you a loser. You can create an environment of learning and giving in a small house, too.

And if your goal is right, a big house doesn't have to make you arrogant or spoiled. You can use it for purposes that are very meaningful.

Food

Food is another way of interacting with the physical world. The same four levels apply: abuse, use, beauty and meaning.

Abuse

The diet industry is a billion-dollar affair. We are all familiar with the abuse of food. People eat when they aren't hungry and eat what isn't healthy. They do it when they know it's destructive. They get mad at themselves for losing control — but they still go after that extra piece of cake. Drug and alcohol abuse is even worse.

Use

What is the practical use of food? Most people would say, only eating what you need and what is healthy so that you have enough energy to do what you want.

Years ago when I was a sophomore in college, two friends and I decided to go on a three-day food fast. All we had was water. Sounds a bit crazy, but we wanted to test our stamina and see how much extra we were eating every day. Mind you, none of us were overweight. It was purely a test of willpower.

Well, the first day was raw torture. All of us wanted to quit, but we figured we would at least get though one full day of fasting. Then we amazed ourselves. The second morning, we weren't even hungry. Everyone went to breakfast in our dormitory. Lunch was comical to us. We laughed at all the people going to the dining room just because it was one o'clock. They were like cows going to graze. They just ate because of the hour and because everyone else was going, too.

I remember thinking how much time people waste in their lives eating, drinking, sleeping and going to the bathroom. Boy was I going to cut down on that stuff!

The third day was a cinch. When it was over, we were actually reluctant to taste anything. We thought we could almost become angels, living on air. The next day I went to a restaurant and had a few hamburgers. I don't remember anything about our experiment after that. I sure lost it fast.

That's the trouble with most physical pleasures. It's very easy to slip into the lower levels, and it takes a certain amount of clarity to turn it around.

By the way, food should not be eaten to the point that

one's stomach is full. During a meal, about one-third less should be eaten than the amount that would fill you up.*

Beauty

The third relationship to food is beauty. You may think, "How can food be beautiful?" Do you remember being away from home for a while? Maybe you were at college or out of town on a job. Then you came home and got a great home-cooked meal! There is something special about it, if the person doing the cooking doesn't look at it as a big hassle.

Nowadays, we're all in a big hurry. We throw a TV dinner into the microwave and wolf it down in five minutes. But good food is a wonderful way to take care of ourselves, or show someone love. It's almost a lost art. I've heard kids say they don't think their parents care about them because they get nothing but fast food dinners, or their family never sits down together at a meal. One way a husband or wife can show their spouse they love them is to prepare a great dinner, or take them out to a good restaurant.

Of course, if it's done with fatty, unhealthy foods, we're back to abusing our bodies. Beauty can enhance pleasure — but if you don't look at the ingredients, it will also enhance blubber.

Meaning

The best way to approach food is through meaning.

Why do you eat? Try asking people this question. They will look at you a little funny. What a silly question, they're thinking. Why do I eat? To stay alive, of course! (That would be level two — eating because it's useful.)

---

*Moses Maimonides (1135–1204), one of the greatest thinkers and physicians of the Middle Ages, wrote this in a medical guide that people follow to this day.

But you persist and say, "No, beyond that. Why do you eat?"

"I guess a good meal makes me feel better about life. Sometimes I feel a bit down and a good meal changes my mood."

Some people will say, "I eat to stay healthy."

There is actually a higher reason for eating. Think of it in terms of a horse and rider.

The rider feeds the horse so it will be strong enough to take him somewhere. Sometimes he may give it sugar to make it happy. But he knows that feeding the horse isn't the *rider's* purpose in life. The rider has a destination and he needs the horse to take him there.

It's the same with food. Our body is a bit like a horse. It takes us where we want to go. We should keep our body healthy, so it can perform for us and help us reach our life goals.

Every person knows that if he doesn't take some kind of reasonable care of his car, it won't last too long. If you know of a gas station that will fill your engine with fuel that will destroy it, will you go there? No way.

We should take at least as good care of our body as we do of our car. Aren't we also using it to take us where we want to go?

And at the very least, we want to spend long, healthy years with our family.

Here is another interesting point about the meaning of food. Kabbalists say that the whole process of eating teaches us valuable lessons about how to become a wise person. Food and wisdom have this in common: they are both meant to nourish. It's just that one nourishes the body and the other the soul.

First, a person should watch what food he puts in his

body. Some things are obviously harmful and no one would think of eating them, like sand or arsenic. The same applies to information. We should be careful about accepting something as fact before we have checked it out carefully.

With food, we chew it into smaller pieces before we swallow it. The same holds for wisdom. Even if an idea is true, we should analyze it bit by bit and not stuff it into our heads like some school kid who just wants the right answer for the test, never mind whether he understands it or not.

After food enters the stomach, it is dissolved and sent on its way to nourish and be assimilated into the body. And — you guessed it — the same applies to wisdom. When we see an idea is true, we should let it become part of our being and live with it.

Some ingredients in the food we digest are useless or even dangerous, so the body excretes it. Once again the same is true of wisdom. If we recognize that part of our information is ineffective or destructive — get rid of it as fast as possible.

Sex

Abuse

First, let's talk about what it means to abuse sex. I'm not talking about rape and brutality. That these things are abusive goes without saying. What I am talking about is someone who seduces another person without caring about that person's feelings.

I remember giving a class to an audience of college students in the early 1980s, when feminism was beginning to take off. One of the guys in the class raised his hand and launched into a five-minute soliloquy on women's rights: how religions of the world have not treated them with enough respect, how they are created equal to man, etc.

As we were walking out of the classroom into the street, he followed me with one of his friends and kept the discussion going. He said he was sick of the way Madison Avenue sells women's bodies, treating them with no respect. Right in the middle of the discussion, he saw a beautiful blonde sitting on the steps of a building we were passing. He turned to his friend and said, "You catch that girl's body? I'm going to try to pick her up!" That ended his idealistic discussion. What struck me was not the fact that he contradicted his previous words and attitude without even breaking stride; rather, it was the ruthlessness I felt in his voice. It is abusive not to care about what you do to another person in order to satisfy your desires.

Use

What about the next level, which is using sex but not abusing it? This would be where the person has some kind of commitment to the other person, doesn't want to hurt them and even cares about them. But his (or her) overriding goal is his *own* body. He wants to satisfy his desires, not give to the other person.

"Using" can even apply to married people. The husband or wife looks at the other person as a physical object who can satisfy their desire when they initiate sex. But there is little thought of giving.

Years ago when I was a journalist, I went to interview a famous professional football player in the locker room after the game. This fellow had boasted in a magazine article that he had slept with over 200 girls in college. His professors must have had a special bed in the back of each classroom. When did he have time for anything else? In order to get into the locker room, I had to push my way through hundreds of women who were waiting outside for him. They almost tore off *my* clothes as I tried to squeeze through.

I went to his locker and began the interview. The truth is, he was a really nice person. A well-known quarterback from an opposing team said the week before that he wouldn't want his kids to be influenced by this guy. When I told him the quote from the quarterback, he was genuinely hurt. "How can he say that?" he asked. "He must be referring to my lifestyle. Maybe he thinks I just dump people and take advantage of everyone. I honestly wouldn't want to hurt another person. Sometimes, I don't even want to do anything with a girl. You won't believe this, but they force themselves at me. A lot of times I'm just really tense and need a way to relax."

I looked at him closely. He wasn't kidding. Some people are such great salesmen, they can sell a drowning man water. This guy really was nice. He just used sex. He really didn't want to abuse anybody.

People sometimes feel they are being treated as an object during sex. There doesn't seem to be any beauty or love. It's not a matter of abuse; the other person just has a need and it's being filled. Let's see what sex would be like on a higher level.

Beauty

People often talk about the beauty of physical relations. They often mean lust rather than anything aesthetic. When a person is truly in love, however, sex enhances the feeling of the beauty of life. Have you ever had the experience of taking a walk somewhere with the one you love? The whole day seems different: the sky, the trees, the people in the street. Everything comes alive! You feel a unity with the world around you. That's an aesthetic experience. I'm not saying a person can always have that. But with the right attitude, it always adds a bit of color and happiness even if the intensity isn't what it could be.

Meaning

The highest level of relating to sex is meaning. Meaning is, "I really love this person. I am giving pleasure, it deepens our relationship." If a primary focus is giving to the other person by showing commitment and caring, it will intensify a couple's bond.

Commitment means permanence — which is more meaningful than beauty. Beauty is fickle and less important when storm clouds enter the horizon.

Kabbala points to a male and female aspect in the way God relates to man. The male aspect is power, the female is more one of envelopment and love. (Thus women, not men, have a womb. In a real sense, they physically surround and give care to another being.)

God's presence encircles us gently, as we feel when we are hiking in a wooded valley on a summer day.

When a man gives flowers to a woman, he is saying, "Let's share the beauty of life." That is the beauty connection to sex. On a deeper level, with proper intention and consciousness, it can become, "Let's feel God's presence together. Your being with me helps me do that." This brings us into the realm of holiness, which occurs when the physical has been lifted into a higher purpose than immediate gratification.

A permanent relationship reinforced by physical love helps us feel the love and security of a connection with God. That's one of the benefits of sex.

I read a study in which women were asked what aspect of sex they enjoyed the most. They said being held and cuddled. To me, this shows that they care about the closeness and reassurance of the relationship the most. How spiritual the world can be for those who share this bond!

I love feeling this emotion. When I was engaged to Sheryl, my wife, I flew to Connecticut to meet her family. We stopped off in New Haven and took a walk on the campus of Yale University. It was late autumn, and the wind was blowing her hair as we strolled around the campus. It was like a scene out of a movie. I remember thinking, "Wow! I'm walking around campus with the woman I'm about to marry. It just doesn't get any better than this."

Women have a special gift for helping men feel this. A man is more apt to be caught in his ambitions and ego and forget to experience the wonderfulness of life that surrounds him. A woman has the power to lift him out of this so that he can become a giver who is fervently aware of his own spirituality. This is one of the great powers of the feminine mystique. Sadly, it has been abused.

It is not wrong for a woman to want to look beautiful, to dress up and wear jewelry. If she is doing it to manipulate a man for wrong motives, or if a man takes unfair advantage of her, then they have descended into the level of abuse.

If she is lifting him into spirituality by pulling him out of his ego and into higher types of consciousness, it is a holy and wonderful thing.

By the way, even if it's just to deepen their commitment to one another and share a moment of warmth, it's also pretty darn good. Everything doesn't have to be on such a high level.

Sex is a very powerful drive and nothing seems to be more exploited nowadays. It can sell cars or help us feel sanctity. Just as dynamite can create roads through mountains, so can sex break through the hardest emotional barriers. But be careful — explosives treated casually are more likely to maim than to build anything permanent.

Travel

So far, we have seen three examples: houses, food and sex. Let's take a look at another — travel. This time, see if you can go through the process yourself.

Let's take a vacation — "going on holiday" as the Europeans call it. Here are the four ways a person can experience it.

1. Abuse

2. Use

3. Beauty

4. Meaning

Now, fill in three ways someone could do each of them:

Abuse:

1. _____

2. _____

3. _____

Use:

1. _____
2. _____
3. _____

Beauty:

1. _____
2. _____
3. _____

Meaning:

1. _____
2. _____
3. _____

At one time or another in our lives, most of us have experienced all of these categories on our vacations. Remember: the goal is to get the most pleasure we can when we travel, which means planning ahead and knowing what we really want.

Let me show you what my list looks like:

Abuse

Leaving garbage on the ground at national parks

I remember I once took my family to the Everglades in Florida. We drove all the way down to the Gulf of Mexico, to what we thought would be an isolated place.

Boy, we were naive. We parked our car a half a mile from the water and entered a little wooded area with beautiful walking paths. But all the way to the beach, we saw beer cans and Coca-Cola bottles.

On another vacation, I was on a bus ride to Granada, Spain. The scenery along the way was beautiful. Lunchtime came, and some of the people pulled out bags of food and started eating. When they finished, they rolled down the windows — and threw the bags out onto the road!

A place to avoid dealing with problems

I'm not referring to a place to relax. Relaxation is a good thing (if not overdone), and all of us need it. Rest and relaxation fall under the next category, "Use."

Escape applies whenever, instead of looking for solutions to problems, we hot tail it in the other direction.

I had a friend in high school whose grandfather left him a piece of land in his will. Whenever he would get into an argument with his parents, he would take a tent and sleeping bag, food for a couple of days and a radio. Then he would hitchhike to his few acres and camp out. The threat was — "Do what I want or I'm not coming home." It was his weapon to get his way. If his parents were destructive and beat him, I could understand. But this was a little unfair.

I haven't seen him for years, but I know he eventually got married and had kids. I hope he doesn't do it to them, too.

A place to cheat on a wife or husband

We're talking about a vacation away from family to have a tryst.

I don't think this needs too much commentary. I'm not trying to push my values on anyone, but I would like to make one point. Sooner or later, most spouses find out. From then on, every time the person who is cheating leaves the house, his or her spouse gets to wondering about where they are headed. Not a great way to have a peaceful home.

Use

Rest and relaxation

This is what many people do on their vacations. It might be combined with a little sightseeing, too. By the way, there is nothing wrong with a vacation combining use, beauty and meaning.

I have a friend, Jeff, who owns a beautiful boat and keeps it anchored in the Bahamas. A few years ago, he invited my wife and me to fly to Freeport and stay on his boat. We took him up on it. We left our kids with friends and took a three-day vacation, our first trip alone in years.

We arrived late afternoon, had a wonderful meal and walked around the city. Then we came back to the boat and went to sleep.

When I awoke in the morning, everyone was already eating breakfast. Jeff took us out to a small, uninhabited island and we went snorkeling. Then he pulled out some lawn chairs and we sat on the beach. That was good for twenty minutes, but I began to get a little restless.

"Jeff," I said, "why don't we explore this island?"

"Go right ahead," he said. "But can I make a suggestion?"

"Of course."

"The reason I invited you out here, is that you're always pushing yourself hard. I thought you needed to lie around for a day or two and do absolutely nothing."

"Nothing? I'll go crazy."

"Well, okay, but I think you'll go sane."

"What do you mean?"

"Look, Tom, you need to relax more. It will refresh you. Are you aware of the sounds around us right now?"

"What sounds?" I said. I listened for a minute. "Oh, you mean the birds?"

"Yes, and the fish jumping out of the water and the waves rolling in. Do you hear the rustling of leaves in the trees behind us?"

I looked at him and laughed. "Wow, I see what you mean. I'm as taut as the strings on a tennis racket."

"You know," said Jeff, "I come out to these islands every four or five months. I don't do anything. Sometimes I put out a big, white towel and lay on the beach for hours. I know I'm finally relaxed when I can watch a bird hopping along the sand for a while, look at my watch and see that two hours have passed."

Relaxation can be wonderful. It clears out the noisy, distracting clutter of our busy lives.

Looking for business opportunities

You might say, what kind of vacation is this? But I have seen people do it many times. I know a businessman who left Czechoslovakia and moved to Canada in the middle 1980s. He built up a sizable fortune in Canada. Then he started going back to Central Europe, buying up businesses.

He told me he would take his vacations there, too. He would go with his wife and young child and travel as far east as Poland. He combined rest and relaxation with keeping his eyes open for some new company he could snap up.

Study

One great way to learn about nature or foreign countries is to go there. When I graduated university, I bought a railway pass for Europe. It allowed me to travel relatively cheaply on trains over much of the continent. I did it for the summer and had one of the greatest times of my life.

One of the things I got from the trip was an understanding of Western history. I sure did get a lot of useful information. When I went back to the United States, I worked as a journalist with the Detroit News. My summer travels taught me how to establish quick rapport with people from different backgrounds and countries — and this in a Midwestern city like Detroit.

Beauty

Inspiration

I remember the first time I visited Florence, Italy. All the buildings and houses had red roofs. It must have been a law there. The architecture of many of the public places dated from the Renaissance. It was simply gorgeous. I loved walking down the streets, staring at the facades.

Think of all the beautiful places people go to in the United States. Our national parks — Yellowstone, Rocky Mountain, Bryce Canyon and many others — lift people emotionally. They remind us how magnificent life really is.

Adventure

I went rafting down the Jordan River in Israel in the summer of 1996. My kids were with me. Though the river is pretty quiet by American standards, we laughed with glee every time we came to rapids.

I classify this with beauty, because both of them lift us out of a mundane feeling toward life.

Wouldn't you love to travel down the Amazon River, or go on a safari to Kruger National Park in South Africa? Think of all the different species of animals and birds you'd see in the wild, or the excitement (from the safety of a barrier) of hearing lions roar at night! These adventures aren't dangerous and they lift us into feeling how wonderful life is.

Let me tell you an adventure I once had. I went mountain climbing outside Barcelona, Spain. I was with a friend from England. We started at dawn. The trails were a bit steep and by early afternoon we were tired. Suddenly we came to a flat plateau spotted with trees and a little stream.

We sat down by the water to eat lunch. I was looking around, admiring the view of the slopes ahead of us, when the Englishman said to me, "Tom, look over there for a second."

He was pointing at clods of manure.

"Must be cows," I ventured.

"But why would cows be up here?" he asked.

"Well, there's a lot of grass and a nice stream. Some shepherd probably brought them."

"But how? And how will he get them down?"

We started walking across the plateau, heading for where the mountain sloped up again. Then we saw them. There were five in all and they weren't cows. They were bulls! Angry looking ones! A few days before, I had gone to a bullfight and saw what those guys could do to a person. The matador had tripped and fallen to the ground. As he stood up, the bull hit him head on and gored its horn into the matador's belly. Other matadors got the bull away and the wounded fighter was carried out of the arena. The next day I read that he had died.

So when I saw those bulls in the distance about a football field away, I ran toward a clump of boulders and scrambled up as fast as I could. My English friend almost burst a gut laughing – until the bulls charged toward him. A few seconds later he was panting beside me. We stayed for a half-hour until the bulls left.

If I had put my life in danger on purpose, we would be talking about the first category: abuse.

There was really no danger here, however, because the bulls couldn't reach us. But it gave us a feeling about the value and beauty of life. Even a little danger wakes us up to how lucky we are to be alive. Adventures help us feel the rich potential of life experiences that are out there for us, and remind us that life is full of awe and excitement.

Museums

This is another way to experience beauty on a trip. Most large cities have art and historical museums. Not everyone likes to go. I used to enjoy it more than I do now, but I still occasionally visit one when I am sightseeing.

Meaning

This is the greatest of the four categories. Using the world and seeing its beauty are good. But they are nothing like the lift that comes from feeling yourself grow as a human being.

Spending time with people we love

Vacations and travel are great chances for spending quality time with family and friends. I once asked my kids to make a list of their five best memories. All of them included trips we had taken across America. We did things we really enjoyed. Best of all for children, there were no distractions that took Daddy's mind somewhere else.

I remember taking a day trip with an old friend. He and I had gotten on bad terms. We took a long walk around a lake, then trekked to a small, rural town. Sharing the experience was helpful for our relationship. It didn't fully heal the problem by itself. We had to talk things out more, but it was a big help that we were sharing peaceful surroundings together.

Widening our horizons

I don't mean learning new facts. I listed that under "Use," like the time I went to Europe and learned a lot of geography and history, which was valuable in my job as a journalist. I mean seeing new faces and cultures that make us reflect upon the way we live, and challenge our view of the universe.

This is one of the reasons people want to travel, whether they are conscience of it or not. They want to lift out of the commonplace details taking up their lives and get a fresh perspective.

They are more open when they travel because they have temporarily left their old habits behind.

Sometimes the change can be so abrupt, the traveler gets a culture shock, as for example when he goes from a Western to a Moslem country. One time I was traveling on a train in Turkey. I was twenty-three years old and the only Westerner in a compartment with three Moslems. Suddenly, they prostrated themselves and started praying. I was surprised at their lack of embarrassment. In Turkey, it was an accepted thing. In America, people would think of calling in the guys with the white coats.

I have a friend who spent several years traveling

around Africa. He went to a small village in Milawe. People accepted him like an old friend. He stayed there for weeks, living by fishing and eating fruit off the trees. He loved the simplicity of the people and their wonderful sense of community.

I am not saying that people should quit their jobs and move to the middle of Africa, but traveling does help us rethink the stereotypical ways in which we relate to life. When my friend returned to the United States, he made sure he found a community where people felt close to each other. (He even became religious.)

Having a spiritual experience

Whether you call it feeling God's presence, or feeling Oneness or whatever words you want to use, traveling can lift us into a transcendental experience. In all the years that I have spent studying religion and mysticism, one of the most powerful experiences I have ever had was when I piled my family into a van and traveled across America from Washington, D.C. to Los Angeles. We went to places like the Grand Canyon and Rocky Mountain National Park. It's not hard to feel the sense of being part of something much greater than ourselves in amazing places like these.

The immense pleasure we feel at such times comes because the Spirit has lifted the Animal Soul into awe. If the Animal Soul didn't feel it, the experience would be about as inspiring as a flat tire.

Types of People

All these activities in the physical world can be experienced on the four levels that I have already described:

abuse, use, beauty and meaning. If you live all of the time on any of these levels, you will become one of the following types of people:

1. *The abuser*

2. *The pragmatist*

3. *The poet*

4. *The spiritual/holy person*

In other words, if you consistently experience life the first way, if that is how you process information, you will become an abuser — in food, travel, sex, etc.

If you only look for the usefulness in everything (level two), you will become a practical person — to the exclusion of other ways of experiencing.

If you always try to go after beauty, you will develop into the "poet" personality.

And if you only go after meaning, you become the spiritual, or holy person.

We are combinations of these four types, hopefully mostly the second, third and fourth.

If we want the greatest pleasures in life, it pays to move away from the abuser and up the ladder. This is not to say that there is not a time and place to act like a pragmatist — for example, when we are fixing a leaky pipe. At such moments, we should focus more on usefulness and less on meaning. But let's make sure that we get the poet and the spiritual side into our lives, too.

Why We Were Put into this World

One motivation to choose the highest levels is to re-member why, according to Kabbala, we have been put in a physical world at all. Why should the soul be placed in a world of trees, mountains, cities and people? What's the point of it all? If we keep the answer in mind, we will choose the most productive strategies in life.

As I said before, the soul contains all wisdom. But at first, this wisdom is abstract. It's like the difference between *reading* about a baseball game versus *playing* in one. If you only get it from books, it's not so real.

When I was in junior high school, I knew someone who grew up in a neighborhood where he had no friends. He never played sports, but he watched them on television. Then he moved onto my block. I was fourteen years old when he came. After a couple of weeks, he joined in a football game we were playing in the street. On the very first play, he ran straight ahead and caught a pass from the quarterback. Then he stopped dead in his tracks. We were playing touch football and somebody caught him. His team went nuts. "Why didn't you keep running?" they yelled at him. He looked down at the pavement and said, "I've only watched football on TV, I never played before so I didn't know what to do."

He never made that mistake again.

Experience makes things much more real. Before the soul comes into this world, all its wisdom is abstract. Then it enters a body, a machine that has eyes, ears, hands and legs. At first, the soul forgets its wisdom — the baby's brain is just too underdeveloped to handle it all.

Then the baby starts to mature into a child who sees something, reflects and *remembers* what he already vaguely knows inside. Now the information becomes real.

Everything around us — trees, mountains, birds, the sun — has meaning. Nature's purpose is to inspire the soul to reflect upon these images and awaken the wisdom inside. Ants, for example, can teach an aspect of humility — each one knows its job and does it without hoarding power for itself. Wisdom thus becomes part of a person's character, rather than being like an unread book packed away in an attic.

Experience in life also helps us know about different emotions — such as love — toward a spouse, a child or a friend. Someone who only reads about love won't fully grasp it. Our time spent in this world gives us the chance to take such emotions out of the realm of abstraction and make them real. And we will carry this wisdom with us for eternity. According to Kabbala, it will teach us how to reach the heights of our potential and experience joy and meaning forever.

If we remember this, we will often be motivated to strive for the highest of the four levels — beauty and spirituality — and avoid the destructiveness of abuse.

\\\\\\\\\\\\\\\\\\\\\\\\\\\\\\

Here is a new question that will help us learn how to empower the Spirit: Where does the wisdom of the Spirit come from?

Have you ever wondered about this? When you ask yourself a question, is the answer already sitting somewhere waiting to be summoned?

In order to find out, we're going to meet the third soul.

THE THIRD SOUL AND THE MIND

One grain of pepper is better than a basketful of gourds (a sharp, reasoning mind is better than a mind full of facts).
Talmud Bavli, Megillah, 7a

SO FAR, WE HAVE TALKED ABOUT THE TWO LOWER links on the necklace of the soul. The first one is the Animal Soul. According to Kabbala, it rests in the liver. The next link, the Spirit, has free will and all good character traits. It makes us specifically human and rests in the heart.

Now we come to an even higher soul — the third, called the *Neshama*, or *Neshama Elyona* in Hebrew. It literally means "breath" and is often translated as the *Upper Soul*. It resides in the brain.

If we make destructive choices and give in to the impulses of the Animal Soul, we actually drive the Upper Soul out of the body. It never completely departs, but sends down an influence like a light drizzle that barely waters the crops below.

The Upper Soul provides awareness, intellectual direction and inspiration. In its greatest moments, it brings us God-consciousness and prophecy. It does this through the mind.

In order to understand how this works, we need to know what the mind is and how to use it. And so, in this section, we will be talking about the powers of the mind. The most important ones are:

Memory

Imagination

Perception

Reason

Memory

Without memory, we'd be lost. We wouldn't recognize our families or remember the training we receive for our jobs.

It's invaluable to imput accurate information into the mind and be able to recall it.

The memory doesn't critically examine information, it just absorbs zillions of bits of it. When we ask it to, it brings the data up. The better one's memory, the better the feedback.

If we get a fact wrong, it becomes part of the memory like a coffee stain in a shirt. We may never clean it out. Instead, we endlessly quote it like a parrot. That's why it's always important to carefully check our facts and opinions before we file them into our heads. Bad entries load us up with distortions and prejudices.

Imagination

The imagination can be used to break up a rigid thought process, so that we can look at something creatively and in a fresh way.

In the early days of television, advertisers didn't quite know how to get the most out of the new medium. Commercials usually consisted of a talking salesman whose words also appeared on the screen. That's because they were still using the techniques of radio and newspapers. Soon a new generation of commercials appeared that made full use of the visual power of television.

That's what the imagination does — it creates a new way of looking at things.

The imagination can be used for humor and fastasy. For example, let's say I ask you to visualize a frog with Groucho Marx eyebrows and a moustache. He's holding a cigar and puffing on it, sending up a cloud of smoke. This frog says, "You know, I'd horsewhip you if I had a horse."

The image is absurd, of course. This leads us to an important lesson: imagination can be used for escape, which is good if it relaxes us and soon afterwards we come back to reality, but bad if we never return to *terra firma*.

The imagination is helpful, therefore, when it leads to creative solutions, but frightening when it leads to delusions.

Perception

The third power of the mind is perception. When you look through a pair of binoculars, wherever you turn them, that's what you see. In the case of perception, whatever we turn our five senses toward is what we "see." The ears hear things. The nose smells things. The eyes do their job. The senses bring in the information and the mind processes it.

Perception is turned on when we are awake. When we are asleep and dreaming, the imagination is in charge. We can also perceive our surroundings when we're asleep. Tests show that if a window is opened near a bed in the winter, the sleeper will often pull his blanket tightly around himself without awakening.

If a person is not thinking about anything but just moving around on automatic pilot, he is still perceiving. He can sit and watch a television program and think of nothing. He is not examining what the program is saying. He is perceiving, nonetheless.

Let's say a person gets up from the television and walks outside. He stares at houses, trees, someone mowing the lawn. He is, of course, using his perception, although he may *still* be acting like a zombie on automatic pilot.

Then he goes for a drive in the countryside. It is an extremely hot day. In the distance, it looks like there is water on the road. He begins to think, "How can that be? There's not a cloud in the sky. It must be an illusion. It's heat rising off concrete, which looks like water but isn't."

This last activity of thought was something more than perception. It was the use of reason, which is the fourth power of the mind and the most important.

Reason

Reason enables us to examine information by looking at it logically and intellectually. If we were to just use the third part of the mind — perception — we would walk around all day like a camcorder. We often do this anyway, hurrying from place to place without thinking about the world around us.

When we use our reasoning ability and combine it with perception, we actually feel an expansion of awareness. We notice much more in life, and think about what we see.

We even experience *ourselves* differently, because we become more conscious of our feelings and actions. Reason alone won't do it, nor will perception alone, but the two together are a powerful combination.

Expand Your Mind

A person without perception is like a television that's turned off. The screen is simply black.

Perception, however, isn't enough. Perceptions must be processed and evaluated. This is done through the use of the reasoning faculty of the mind.

Using perception without reason is like a television that's turned on, but getting white static or random, disconnected pictures.

Whenever I get really spaced out, my wife Sheryl says, "Earth to Tom, Earth to Tom" and we both break out in a laugh. At such times, my perception is working fine but I'm blanked out by daydreaming.

Reason doesn't necessarily mean analyzing through logic, but can be simply paying attention to something. You could be noticing a bird, the teacher writing on a blackboard, or the scenery rushing by as you sit in a car. But you are focused on what you are experiencing, and not just staring out into space.

Sometimes I take walks with my daughter Devorah. I love going with her because she knows everything that's happening in the neighborhood.

"Dad, do you see the broken pipe on the side of that house? It burst yesterday and flooded the yard. Do we have any bad pipes?"

"Look at that old tree. There are two birds' nests up there with babies."

"See that little girl with the curly brown hair? She's trying not to suck her finger. I bet she made a deal with her Mom that she gets something if she breaks the habit. Why don't we try that with Benjamin?"

All of which I would never notice on my own.

If a person gets really good at working with perception and reason, he begins to notice many things indeed. He gets a rush from the beauty and the spirituality around him. The whole world seems to come alive. He picks up much more information coming in through his senses — sounds, smells, sights. He becomes aware of his own inner feelings and those of others.

He understands things he never understood before.

This is what we call "mind expansion," a phrase made popular in the 1960s.

We'll talk more about awareness and mind expansion in Chapter 12, and explain how to do it. But first, it's necessary to know more about the mind itself.

Five Types of Knowledge

We use the powers of the mind to know many things. There are of course billions and billions of things to know. How far away is that car which is moving toward me?

How much is six times five? What is the definition of justice? What will happen if I call my mother up and tell her I am engaged?

All these bits of information fall into general categories of knowledge. I'm going to explain the five that are most commonly used.

The first category I call *sensory information*. These are things we know from our five senses: taste, touch, sight, smell and hearing.

It is very important to trust sensory information, otherwise we won't walk out of the way of a car moving toward us, or we'll think that the ground in front of us is teeming with alligators. We won't even believe that we're awake or the sky is blue.

How do I know my mother is calling me? Because I trust my hearing.

We use the brain to collect this sensory information. Then we make a judgment about what it means.

The next category of knowledge is *logic*. Here is an example: if I start out with the premise that most people living in the United States speak English, and I find out that you live there, then it is logical to say that you probably speak English.

Of course, the conclusion will be wrong if the premise is off. If instead I were to say that *every* person living in the U.S. speaks English, and since you live there you must speak it too — that could very well be wrong. What if you recently moved there from China and don't know the language? We must do the best we can to make sure our premises are correct. Then logic will work for us.

Another type of knowledge is called *projection.* Projection helps me predict something which is going to happen in the future. For example, let's say I invent the following scenario: this afternoon I am going to call up my wife and tell her, "Honey, I've decided to quit my job, sit on a street corner and beg for food." She will say to me, "Either you're joking, going through a mid-life crisis or 100% nuts."

This ability of the mind to put together the future is called projection. It's not an exact science. My wife *could* say, "Great idea! I want to come with the kids." She could say that, but the odds are pretty slim.

Projection uses the imagination combined with reason.

Another type of knowledge is called *moral* — deciding whether your behavior is right or wrong, decent or indecent. People like to say this is not knowledge at all, but entirely societal-based and without any root in objectivity. But it really isn't so.

In one of Plato's Dialogues called *Meno,* his teacher, Socrates, shows that human beings have mathematical concepts imprinted in their souls. He uses a slave to illustrate his point. The slave, in answering a series of logical questions from Socrates, discusses difficult principles in geometry that he never could have studied before or thought about on his own. Socrates says that his questions are causing the slave to search inside for what is already there.

Kabbala teaches that, in the same way, we have complex moral information embedded in our souls. The information is sitting there, ready to be retrieved.

Let's take the following as an example: is it ok to say bad things about someone behind his or her back? Is there anything wrong with saying, 'Dick and his wife aren't getting along. It's really fun watching them scream at each other. You know what he said to his wife last night? He told her that she's an idiot and he wants a divorce!'"

Ask people if there is anything wrong with talking like that. Ask them if there is anything wrong with talking viciously about the personal lives of the people in their offices or neighborhoods. Many people *do* it, of course, because we are frail human beings with faults. But everyone will say you *shouldn't*.

Now ask them, "Fine, you say it is wrong to gossip. How about if you know that your friend is about to go into business with someone who is a thief? Is it right to warn your friend?" Everyone will say, "Yes, that's ok because you're trying to do the right thing and protect your friend."

Or how about this example: you have a good friend and she's about to get engaged. The guy has violently beaten every girl he's gotten close to. You even know that he was married twice and regularly beat both wives. Is it right to warn your friend? Everyone will say yes.

So now we have two principles. One principle is, it's wrong to gossip when there is no decent purpose. The second principal is that saving someone from financial or physical abuse is a decent purpose. You will find that everyone you ask comes to the same conclusion. I could give thousands of other examples.

It is true that people disagree on a lot of moral issues. That's because some of these issues are complex and hard to sort out. Furthermore, rather than reasoning through the steps, people throw back answers they accepted years before without critically examining them. In other words, they are using memory rather than reason.

Or their Animal Soul has a strong, pressing desire that distorts their judgment. If people can make good money on a business deal, for example, it sometimes becomes difficult to talk to them about right and wrong. In the early 1900s, the contents of food packages were not listed. Sanitary inspections of food packing and processing plants were rare. The motto in business was *"Let the buyer beware"* — this meant that it was up to consumers to find out about what they were eating, and not the obligation of companies to tell them.

It took a few major scandals and a book by Upton Sinclair to change all that. In *The Jungle,* Sinclair described the horrors of the meat-packing industry in Chicago. An outraged and disgusted public pressed Congress to pass stiff legislation.

For the sake of money, the Animal Soul had gotten these industrialists to rationalize. "It's not our responsibility to be careful about what we put in our products," they said. "We're not *forcing* anyone to buy them."

There are a lot of desires that make us rationalize and block out moral knowledge — money, sex and power to name a few. The information remains in the soul, waiting for us to retrieve it; but we have to *want* to.

The next type of knowledge is called **meaning**. This involves information that gives purpose and value to people's lives. It could help them understand themselves better, improve their relationships or help them become more spiritual.

Ask someone which is more meaningful, the number of bumps on the ceiling or his relationship with his children. I don't think any normal person will say the former.

If I talk to a crowd about bumps on a ceiling they will soon fall asleep. If I talk about the behavior of a colony of ants, they'll listen a little longer. The reason is that they feel like they may learn something from ant behavior that will apply to their own lives. (They may not be conscious of this.) As I mentioned before, ants teach about humility – each one does a job helpful to the colony without trying to grab power for itself. And ants store food during the summer so that they won't starve in the winter months.

But what are people going to learn about life from bumps on a ceiling?

I've seen this come up in interviews with scientists. If a scientist is pressed on why he studies ants or black holes, he will often say, "They help us learn more about ourselves and the universe we live in."

I call this type of knowledge "meaning."

There are many other categories of knowledge, but these are the ones we use most often.

Controlling Your Mind

In order to get control of the mind and use it effectively, you have to know which types of knowledge you trust and which types you don't. If information comes in but you think your mind can't get it clear, what good will that do?

Most people trust their sensory input. If they see a car coming they move. They are certain of their judgment. This type of knowledge is critical and fairly straightforward (unless an organ is damaged, like the eyes or ears).

How many times in your life have you doubted that you are awake and not dreaming? Perhaps a few times when you were drowsy, but for the most part you are sure.

People have more difficulty trusting the other types of knowledge. Many people are not good at logic. If you aggressively attack their reasoning process, they will get defensive, or perhaps say "I guess I made a mistake."

Some people are very good at projection. They can see

the future consequences of their actions or of the head-
lines in the daily newspaper. Other people are bad at it.
They actually think that if they come home really late, their
spouse or parent won't be annoyed or ready to call the
police from worry.

Here is a good exercise. Make a list of these types of
knowledge: sensory, logic, projection, moral and meaning. Ask yourself, which ones do you trust and which not?
Next to the ones where you don't have confidence, ask
why not.

	Trust	*Don't Trust*	*If Don't Trust, Why Not?*
Sensory			
Logic			
Projection			
Moral			
Meaning			

Here are three reasons people don't trust their mind:

• **Lazy Thinking**

They just aren't used to using their mental muscles in
certain areas like logic. Some people are gifted at logic,

but others get frustrated quickly. Instead of thinking an idea through step-by-step, they go the easy way and follow an impulse.

The other day, I was talking to a girl about marriage. She asked me, "How do you know when you are in love with someone?" I said to her, "Well, first you have to know what you mean by love."

"What are you talking about?"

"Do you agree that if a guy is just interested in a woman's body and doesn't return phone calls the minute he gets what he wants, that's not love?"

"Yes, but there are also women who do that to men."

"You're right, of course there are," I said. "And that's not love either."

"If women do it too, maybe that's just the way people are. Do you really believe you can ever love anybody?"

"Let's try to define love so we don't get it mixed up with something else."

"You can't define it," she interrupted. "It's an emotion, it's spontaneous."

"Have you ever tried to define it?" I asked.

"No."

"Then how do you know you can't? Someone who had a great influence on my life* defined it this way: 'Love is the pleasure you get when you see someone's good qualities.'"

"What if I love someone but he doesn't have any good qualities?"

"Then what are you loving?"

"I might love being able to take care of him."

---

*That "someone" is Rabbi Noah Weinberg, whom I referred to in an earlier footnote.

"That doesn't mean you love *him*. You love feeling useful."

"I once helped someone a lot," she said. "But he didn't appreciate it at all."

"Did you feel love for him?"

"No, I didn't. That proves what I'm saying."

"How?" I asked.

"I'm not sure. What point are we discussing, anyway?"

She was staring at me blankly. That's when I realized she couldn't reason step-by-step. What she could do was throw monkey wrenches in my statements.

The reason she wasn't very good at logic is that *she wasn't used to using it.* Discussions with people who don't trust logic can require extra patience before you understand each other.

• **Social Pressure**

Did you ever know something was wrong, yet follow the crowd?

You may even forget you are doing it until years later when you think, "What's happened to me? Why have I given up my own judgment for other people's approval?"

We often think that young people are the ones most subject to peer pressure. But how many of our own opinions are molded by the media, friends or coworkers? Most people in the United States who lived north of the Mason-Dixon Line were against slavery in the 1860s. Most people south of it were pro-slavery. Why? Did the air change and affect their judgment when they crossed state lines, or was it social pressure?

Here is another example: many college students in the 1960s used to say, "I don't believe in absolute morality. There is no such thing as right and wrong, it's all subjective." If you waited ten minutes and asked them, "Do you think someone should get paid less money at a job because he is black?" — they would say, "Certainly not, that's racist and evil."

Evil? Didn't they say there is no such thing as absolute morality? But there was social pressure in America to say that racism is immoral, *and* social pressure to say that morality is subjective. So they held two conflicting ideas without noticing it.

Even perceptual knowledge can be distorted by social pressure. Some psychologists at Yale University once did an experiment. They took a bunch of students, showed them a rod that was one foot long, and told them to exaggerate its length when they would be called on in a test situation. Some of them were told to say it was 1¾ of a foot long, and some 2 feet. Then they brought in an unsuspecting student who listened to these people give their prearranged overblown estimates. When they asked him how long *he* thought the rod was, what do you think he said? Almost every poor fellow gave a number from 1¾ to 2 feet! Students who were asked the same question when alone usually got it about right.

This shows that even something as simple as perceptual knowledge can be distorted by social pressure.

- **Fear of Consequences**

There is a third factor that weakens people's ability to get information from their mind: they don't want to hear it because they don't like the consequences. Five plus five equals ten, but the guy behind the cash register in a drugstore might want it to be twelve, and the guy paying might want it to be eight.

This is especially devastating for moral perceptions.

People convince themselves that they are not cheating in business or taking revenge for some remark made to them the day before.

To summarize, there are three ingredients in trusting your mind: don't be a lazy thinker, don't give in to social pressure, and don't be afraid of the consequences of your ideas.

Let me word it positively:

1   *Work hard on your ideas.*

2   *Stand up to social pressure.*

3   *Fearlessly follow your line of reasoning, wherever it leads. (Even if you don't end up acting on it.)*

When you do this often enough, you'll gain supreme confidence in your ability to think and reach sensible conclusions. This, in turn, will empower your third soul.

LIVING WHAT YOUR SOUL KNOWS

> An empty bag cannot stand up-
> right.
> *Ben Franklin, Poor Richard's
> Almanac, January, 1770*

I ONCE ASKED THE FOLLOWING QUESTION AT ONE of my seminars: "Do you believe people are obligated to try to be happy?"

People looked a bit puzzled. "What do you mean by *obligated?*" one woman asked. "You're either happy or you're not."

I had them take a vote. Out of a group of about two hundred people, fifteen raised their hand to say it was an obligation.

"Let me ask you a different question," I said. "If someone is hurting his wife and kids because he is moody and depressed, should he try to do something about it?"

Everyone agreed that he should.

"A minute ago, you said it was not an obligation to try to be happy, but now you're saying that it is. So you have changed your position."

Several people laughed.

Now I turned to two people who had raised their hands at the outset to say that happiness is an obligation. "When you raised your hands, what was your reason?"

"I hadn't really thought it out," said a girl with long red hair. "I just knew that it was very negative to be depressed."

This little story illustrates two levels of knowledge. The first level is a gut feeling that something is true. The girl with red hair had a gut feeling that happiness is an obligation.

The trouble with gut feelings is that they can be wrong.

The second level of knowledge comes from asking the question, "Why do I believe this? What is my evidence?" The evidence in the above case was that if you are unhappy, you might unnecessarily hurt the people around you and that would be wrong.

I call these two levels:

1   Gut feeling

2   Why I believe it

It's invaluable to take your insights to the second level. Anything that remains on the first level will be fuzzy, subject to forgetting and easily demolished by social pressure. If you know what you believe and why you believe it, your knowledge will be pretty unshakable.

There is an even deeper level of knowledge. I call this third level:

3   Realization

Realization is when you not only feel an idea and know why you believe it, but you internalize it. You *live* it. On a gut level, we can know it is important to be happy. We can even work on the "why." But the most important step is to assimilate it into our being and implement what we know.

We know tons of stuff on levels one and two, but fewer things on level three.

Here is a fun exercise. Write down ten things you believe in. As you write down each one, put a check mark next to the level you have it on.

	IDEA	*Gut Feeling*	*I Know Why*	*I Live With It*
1.				
2.				
3.				
4.				
5.				
6.				
7.				
8.				
9.				
10.				

Here's an example of a chart that I made:

	IDEA	*Gut Feeling*	*I Know Why*	*I Live With It*
1.	It's rude to interrupt people		✓	
2.	I love my wife			✓
3.	I should spend more time with my children		✓	
4.	Exercise gives you more energy	✓		
5.	America is a free country			✓
6.	Anger is a waste of time		✓	
7.	I need to know more about computers	✓		
8.	Writing takes discipline		✓	
9.	I'm not going to live forever		✓	
10.	I should try to be a good person			✓

This exercise is very helpful. It shows me why my wife and I have such a great relationship. It also shows me why I am lousy at computers and have put on a few extra pounds lately.

Negative One, Negative Two, Negative Three

We have said that our minds collect all kinds of information and that the information can attain a level of one, two and three. But sometimes we use our minds to get wrong information.

For example, let's say I really dislike Joe. Everything about him irritates me — his voice, his clothes, his posture. One day I'm driving in Joe's neighborhood and happen to pass his house. The lawn hasn't been cut. What's my gut feeling? Joe is a slob and this is just another example of his poor behavior.

Now I bring it to level two. Why do I believe this about Joe? Well, I remember one time he had a big stain on his shirt. And look at that lawn! He's lazy and doesn't care about his neighbors.

Then I bring it to level three. Boy, he irritates me. I decide to let him have it the next time I see him.

The truth is that Joe and his family took a two-week vacation. He gave money to a lawn-mowing company that misplaced his order. It's absolutely not Joe's fault at all.

You can call this "knowledge," all of which is incorrect, levels −1, −2, and −3.

All of our levels of knowledge are either +1, +2, +3 or −1, −2, −3. Many times, the Animal Soul *wants* minuses. It wants excuses to be comfortable and get immediate gratification, so it searches for rationalizations.

The Spirit wants true information.

To make sure we get the right information, we have to be very careful how we ask the mind for answers. If we ask it like an Animal Soul, we're often going to get in trouble. The Animal Soul starts out by saying, "Insofar as Joe is irritating and I'd really like to tell him off, let's keep an eye out for proof of what a slob he is."

Before approaching an issue, it's a good practice to ask yourself, "Where do I *want* the answer to go?" The mind is just a computer. If I ask it to convict Joe, it will. If I ask it to weigh the evidence carefully, it will.

The Talmud puts it this way: "Question witnesses intensively and be cautious with your words lest they learn to lie" (Avos 1:9).

This means that it is not enough to just gather information. You must also be very careful as to how you ask questions, because you might get back what you feel like hearing. This applies to our own minds. If we ask like an Animal Soul, we'll get an Animal Soul answer.

Not only will we get a wrong gut feeling, but also we will become experts at rationalizing it and assimilating it into our character.

If we act like a Spirit, we'll get a Spirit answer.

We all have opinions and beliefs. It's good practice to ask ourselves how we arrived at a particular conclusion. Did we think it out? Did we hear it on the radio? Did we get it from a friend or teacher?

The Absolute Standard

Let's get back to a question I asked earlier: When we are searching inside ourselves for an answer to something, where are we going? Where is all this wisdom *sitting?*

Let's look at a few examples. We've already seen the first one.

1. We've talked about moral knowledge. People will usu-
    ally say, "It's wrong to gossip." Even though they see
    most people doing it, they know it's wrong either be-
    cause they heard this when they were younger, or be-
    cause they came to the realization themselves. But let's
    say you give them the following case: your friend is
    about to get married to a man who has beaten women,
    including two previous wives. You have this informa-
    tion. Should you tell your friend? Most of us would
    say yes. Where are we going inside to get the answer?

2. You're playing left field in a softball game. Someone
    belts a long fly ball over your head. You start gallop-
    ing toward the fence and make a leaping backhanded
    catch. What did you check inside that enabled you to
    know where the ball was going?

3. Let's pretend you live in a society that tells you that
    all people with red skin are devils. You fight off the
    pressure and say, "These people are human beings just
    like us. We don't even know them. If we talk to them
    and treat them decently, we'll see that they have fami-
    lies and dreams and the desire to be good just like
    anybody else." What are you checking that enables
    you to rise above your society and see something like
    this?

In all of the above examples, the answer is what I call
the Absolute Standard. Every human being has an Absolute Standard. In fact, without one, there wouldn't be much
sense in communicating at all.

When we talk to one another, we're either trying to

brainwash the other person, or help him look inside himself and see what *we* are seeing.

That's the difference between education and brainwashing. In education, I am trying to get you to look inside and find the answer that is sitting there, waiting to be discovered. In brainwashing, I don't want you to check inside. I just want to plant information, to jam it into your mind so that it becomes part of your memory without ever being critically examined.

If there were no Absolute Standard, what would be the point of thinking at all? We'd just be turning our wheels or drawing arbitrary solutions.

The Animal Soul has the Absolute Standard. So does the Spirit. The Animal Soul often ignores it and impulsively hurls a desire at the Spirit: "Give me that piece of cake," "Grab that girl," "Hate that person."

The Spirit always wants truth if the Animal Soul doesn't overwhelm it. If it is in charge, you will always use your mind properly. But if the Animal Soul is running the show, you're in big trouble. Sometimes the Animal Soul will be right — if you have trained it to be careful, it will stay away from the extra piece of cake. And it usually wants to catch the baseball — why not, it feels lousy missing the ball and looking like a klutz.

But lots of times it will be wrong due to the reasons I gave earlier: lazy thinking, social pressure and fear of consequences (see Chapter 7).

It's staggering, even awe-inspiring, to recognize that we have truth within us. We can know an endless number of things if we want to.

Albert Einstein is a great example of someone who knew this. His Theory of Relativity revolutionized modern physics, but at first it was controversial. Not only was it disputed, it was pretty darn hard to understand.

One of the implications of the theory is that lightwaves are pulled by gravity. A group of scientists devised a way to check this. A solar eclipse was supposed to occur on a certain day. The scientists set up equipment to see whether the rays of the sun would be bent toward the moon as they passed by on their way to earth.

A reporter came to Dr. Einstein and asked what he would say if the rays did not appear to behave as he predicted.

"I would say that the instruments were faulty," he calmly responded.

He was sure that his mind had gotten the correct answer (in our terms, he had plugged into the Absolute Standard), and he didn't need a physical demonstration to prove it.

By the way, his prediction turned out to be true!

That's what I call trusting your mind — not out of arrogance or stubbornness, but from knowing that you are thinking logically.

Remember to ask yourself, "What do I want the answer to be? Am I prejudiced toward an outcome right from the start?" Then use your mind and trust its conclusions, always keeping an open attitude toward new information.

Without trusting our minds, we become like a computer whose plug has been pulled out of the wall — it can't do anything.

Trusting your mind doesn't mean you are arrogant. Quite the contrary, you are trying to get to the Absolute Standard and sort out reality from illusion. If the car is coming at me, I trust my mind and move out of the way.

We also make moral decisions all the time. We want to get to the Absolute Standard and do what's right, not just rationalize and do what's temporarily comfortable.

Refusing to listen to new information, on the other hand, *does* lead to arrogance and can be deadly.

Don't Be Afraid of Questions

Sometimes we get intercepted by a question that makes us lose confidence in ourselves.

I used to play a game in seminars. I would ask all the participants to write down one idea he or she was willing to defend in front of everybody. I'd ask them to make it as simple as possible. People would pick things like:

"I am awake right now"

"I was born in New York"

"Men have landed on the moon."

"This room is warm."

Then I would ask them to go in front of the room and defend their statements. You might think these are easy things to prove. But just try it sometime.

Let's take the first one — "I am awake right now." A business executive in his forties faced the following barrage of questions:

"How do you know you're awake? Didn't you ever have a dream in which you thought you were awake? It was so real, you actually thought it was happening?"

"Yes."

"Maybe the same thing's going on right now. The dream's so real that you think you're awake."

"This isn't a dream. I know I'm awake."

"How can you be sure? Haven't you ever fooled yourself before? Haven't you ever woken up and thought something you had been dreaming was really happening?"

"This is just different."

"Are you one hundred percent positive? Would you be willing to sign a piece of paper stating that you would give up $5000 if we can prove you're dreaming right now?"

"No, of course not."

"Why not? If you're one hundred percent sure, why wouldn't you sign?"

"I guess I'm not totally sure."

"Then don't say you *know* you're awake. You only *think* you're awake."

This discussion may seem a little silly, but I've seen it happen many times. After all these questions, people lose confidence. This poor fellow still knows he's awake. He's not going to be shaken too much. But when you take really complicated issues (especially when people have something at stake, like in business), things can get shaky very quickly.

Let's take a look at one of the other ideas —"I was born in New York."

"How do you know? You're telling us that you remember your birth?"

"Of course not. But my mother says I was born there."

"When's the last time you asked her?"

"I don't remember when it came up."

"Are you positive she's the one who told you?"

"Pretty much. Someone must have told me. Wait a minute, I have a birth certificate at home."

"Are you telling us no birth certificate has ever been wrong? Have you ever done a study of the percentage of birth certificates that are wrong?"

"No."

"Then how can you tell us you know you were born in New York?"

You get the point. The process a person would normally go through is that he would ask his mind a question, like "How do I know I was born in New York?" The mind would go to the Absolute Standard which would make sure the mind says, "I've been told where I was born by different relatives. I've never heard of a birth certificate being wrong and it certainly can't happen often. It's safe to say that, given all this, I was born in New York."

This would actually incorporate all three levels of knowledge:

1. The person's gut feeling that he was born in New York.

2. A lot of supporting evidence.

3. Assimilation of the information — he unhesitatingly writes down "New York" under "birthplace" on all forms he fills out.

Three Types of Questions

If people wilt under fire when challanged about information as simple as where they were born, imagine how easy it is to lose confidence about truly difficult moral, political and religious beliefs.

There are really only three types of questions that sow doubt in us. When you get hit with one of them, don't panic or get stampeded into dropping your belief. Nor is there any need to become stubborn and hold onto a position without examining it. Just sort out what's being challenged and come to your own conclusion.

Here are the three types of questions:

1. **In Hebrew it's called a *she'eyla*.** Let's say Bob claims that women can't take the pressure of running a large corporation. A *she'eyla* would be, "Bob, what percentage of the work force is female?" That's a simple question — it doesn't challenge his belief.

   Some people get scared right away. They think, "Gee, since I don't know the answer to that, I don't know what I'm talking about at all." Or they think, "Boy, do I look stupid. I really shouldn't have an opinion."

   The important thing to realize about a *she'eyla* is that it never threatens your belief. You could still be right. Don't be embarrassed, just tell the person (including yourself) — "I'm going to go look that up." And do it!

2. **In Hebrew, the second type of question is called a *kashe*.** It means "difficulty." A kashe is a question that points out a contradiction. It demands an answer, but as one of my teachers once said, "No one ever died from a *kashe*."

   For example, a kashe would be, "Bob, if women are incapable of running large companies, why are they heading twenty-six businesses listed on the New York Stock Exchange?" It's still not total proof — maybe the companies are going broke.

3 **The third type of question is called a *tyuvta*.** A *tyuvta* is a knockout blow. It destroys the idea. It proves that the person didn't get his position from the Absolute Standard. A tyuvta in our case would be to show Bob that many of these twenty-six companies on the New York Stock Exchange are doing excellently, and it is

due to their female CEOs. In such a case, he would have to change his opinion.

Summary

The mind is one of our greatest assets. As we undertake our journey through life, our minds provide us with an on-board information system. Imagine entering a spaceship and blasting off without a computer. We wouldn't even drive a car without the information on the dashboard!

Well, we *have* entered a spaceship — our bodies. And we have the greatest computer in existence!

Therefore, it's critical to use our minds with full confidence. Knowing that answers are inside of us is an important step.

The only pitfalls we have to worry about are:

- **Work hard on your ideas**. You'll never understand something if you don't think about it.

- **Stand up to social pressure**. You have a right to your own opinions.

- **Fearlessly follow your line of reasoning, wherever it leads**. Just like it makes sense to pay attention to the gas gauge in a car, it's smart to know reality, even if you don't end up acting on it.

And remember — questions won't kill you. The best scenario is that they'll make you think and grow. The worst scenario is that you'll see you were wrong and have to change your opinion — which will also make you grow.

Now we can begin to experience how the third soul — the Upper Soul — uses the mind to enlighten us. We will do this in the next chapter.

9 TOUCHED BY THE THIRD SOUL

The blossoms appear on the earth,
the time of song is come,
and the voice of the turtledove is heard in our land.

King Solomon,
Song of Songs, Ch. 2:12

WE'VE TALKED A LOT ABOUT THE FIRST TWO SOULS. The Animal Soul resides in all animals, and in human beings too.

The Spirit is above the Animal Soul. It distinguishes man from animals. All good traits come from the Spirit and free will is rooted there.

The Upper Soul is the third soul. When a person has wisdom, good character and is happy, the Upper Soul joins the Spirit and gives it enlightenment and spirituality. It does this through the mind. If a person lacks wisdom, has bad character or is unhappy, the Upper Soul separates from the body and sends its light from a distance.

How should a person behave if he wants to draw down light from the Upper Soul? Let me give an illustration.

A Walk in the Garden

Imagine yourself as a fifty-year-old man. You wake up one morning, get dressed and eat breakfast. You walk out to the mailbox and find a letter saying that you just won $100,000 in the lottery. You yell out a "Yahoo!" and run back in the house to tell your wife. The phone is ringing. It's your daughter on the line.

"Dad," she says, "I'm calling you from school. I thought of you last night. I just want you to know how much I love you and miss you and Mom."

What a morning! Then your wife says, "Why don't we take the day off work and go for a nice drive? I know a beautiful spot by a lake where we can have a picnic together."

So the two of you jump in the car, drive out of the suburbs and go along a narrow highway. Soon your wife tells you to turn onto a dirt road. You feel wonderfully happy today. A windfall check came in, your daughter loves you, your wife's happy to have you to herself, the view is gorgeous and you feel as free as a lark.

"Where are we going?" you ask.

"We're almost there," she says. "Don't be impatient. You're going to love the place."

Finally, you pull off the dirt road into a little clearing. There's no one around. The two of you leave the car and walk for a few minutes until you come to a long, wooden gate. "Let's open the gate and go in," says your wife.

"Maybe it's private property. How do you know we can just enter?"

"Don't be silly," she says. "I talked to the person who owns this place. We're welcome to spend the afternoon here."

So in you go. Your wife closes the gate and it clicks shut. You enter a thicket of woods and walk along the path. The sun is out. Birds are singing in the trees. You let yourself relax and feel the beauty of life. Suddenly, you come to a clearing. When you walk in, it's as if you are entering a different world full of flowers and fruit trees. There is a lake one hundred yards in front of you. Your wife picks some blueberries and you pull an apple off a tree.

"This is so beautiful," you say.

"I know," she says.

She smiles and you suddenly remember how much you love her. The two of you walk to the lake and sit down on the grass. "Is that a fawn I see in the distance?" you ask.

"Isn't it beautiful?" responds your wife. "It's so peaceful here."

The fawn moves toward you.

All the tension leaves your body. The fawn comes, sniffs at you and finally rubs against your side.

"Wow!" you say to your wife. "Where are we?"

"You know," says your wife, "this place isn't really so different from our own backyard. We have apple trees and plenty of flowers. There are always birds there. But there's one thing we didn't bring with us and that's why we're so happy."

"What's that?" you ask.

"Worry!" says your wife. "You had such a great day that you left your worries behind."

\\\\\\\\\\\\\\\\\\\\\\\\\\\\\\\\\\\\\\\

The Upper Soul enlightens us so that we see the holiness and gorgeousness of the world. Anytime I've asked someone what were his or her greatest moments in life, it's been something uplifting like the scene above. These are moments when we feel meaningful and happy. It could be a walk in a beautiful place, being in a delivery room when your baby is born, saving someone's life or being in love.

At such moments, we notice new doors open in ourselves. We become aware of something wonderful and greater than the physical world around us. We rise above pettiness. The mind clears up and the Upper Soul exerts its power.

I'm not talking about hallucinating. If anything, we've never been so clear in our life. We are aware of everything around us. Our mind is alive, our emotions serene and we feel a sense of awe at the universe.

This is what the Upper Soul is able to give us. We drive the Upper Soul out of the body (except for a spark that continues to descend to us) through depression, bitterness and other negative traits, which cloud the mind. Remember — the Upper Soul works through the mind.

We reunite with our Upper Soul through happiness and knowing how to deal with misfortune — which we will discuss in the next two chapters.

10

HAPPINESS

The joy of the heart gives birth
to song.

Zohar 2:93a

IN ORDER FOR THE UPPER SOUL (THE THIRD SOUL)
to lift us into awareness and inspiration, it's got to have
fuel. Happiness is the fuel.

Happiness is like gasoline in an airplane. Take it away
and nothing gets off the ground.

Happiness has two time frames, the present moment
and the future.

Some of the spiritual gurus advise people to live only
in the present. If we would just live in the "now" and not
think about the future, they say, life would be bliss. But
I've found that doesn't really work. People think lots about
the future and they should.

On the other hand, if you *only* think about the future,

you're never going to enjoy what's right under your nose.

I once had a friend who took a vacation with his family to Hawaii. When he got back, I asked him how it went.

"Lousy," he said.

"How could a trip to Hawaii be lousy?"

"All I ever did was take photographs," he said. "I got three albums out of it, but I barely relaxed for a moment."

That's what you call living in the future.

So we're going to focus on how to achieve both present-moment happiness and joy about the future.

Happiness

Let's start out with how to be happy in the present moment. I'm going to give an assignment, which I really encourage you to do. The results will be fun and surprising.

Make a list of 25 things you think you need in order to be totally happy. Don't censor yourself, just write freely without worrying about how your list looks.

LIST A

1. _____
2. _____
3. _____
4. _____
5. _____
6. _____
7. _____
8. _____
9. _____
10. _____
11. _____
12. _____
13. _____
14. _____
15. _____
16. _____
17. _____
18. _____
19. _____
20. _____
21. _____
22. _____
23. _____
24. _____
25. _____

Here are some things people often put on their lists at my seminars:

1   *One million dollars*

2   *One billion dollars*

3   *Sex with ten Hollywood Stars*

4   *A six-month cruise around the world*

5   *To be President of the United States*

6   *A Porsche*

7   *The perfect marriage*

8   *To be famous*

9   *To have my own TV show*

10   *Healthy children*

11   *Parents that get along*

12   *A mansion*

13   *My own private jet*

You've got to admit, this is some basket of goodies.

What Is Happiness?

I think this is a good time to define our subject:

Happiness means taking pleasure in what you have.

You're certainly not going to be happy about the things you don't have. Happiness is when you walk outside on a beautiful summer day, look around and suddenly feel a rush of pleasure. Or when you come home from work and your child runs to greet you at the door.

When you sit down to a great meal at a fancy restaurant, you definitely feel good. That's because you're happy — you're enjoying what you have.

Yet look at the things that appear on people's lists. One fact is clear: if they want to be happy, they are going about it the wrong way. They are focusing on what they *don't* have. If most of their attention is directed toward what they don't have, are they going to be happy? Of course not. I'm certainly not saying that they shouldn't strive for all those things. But they also should take pleasure in what's in their own backyard.

Look at your own list. How many of the things on it do you presently have? If only a few of them or even none, then you're saying, "My happiness depends on getting X, Y and Z." I certainly hope you get them. But what about being happy in the meantime?

What I want you to see is that you already have many wonderful blessings. It's enriching and productive to notice them.

Therefore, I want you to make another list. This time, write down twenty five of the greatest blessings you currently have in your life.

LIST B

1. _____
2. _____
3. _____
4. _____
5. _____
6. _____
7. _____
8. _____
9. _____
10. _____
11. _____
12. _____
13. _____
14. _____
15. _____
16. _____
17. _____
18. _____
19. _____
20. _____
21. _____
22. _____
23. _____
24. _____
25. _____

These are some of the things people commonly put on their lists:

1 *I have hands*

2 *I have feet*

3 *I have eyes*

4 *I have ears*

5 *My parents are alive*

6 *One of my parents is alive*

7 *I am alive*

8 *I have children*

9 *I have a good friend*

10 *I own my house*

11 *I love my wife or husband*

12 *My wife or husband loves me*

13 *I learn something new every day*

14 *I know how to read and write*

15 *I live in America, Canada, etc.*

16 *I am relatively sane*

Now you have two lists:

- **The things you need in order to be happy**
- **The blessings you already have.** You may not have all of the things on list B, but I'm sure you have some of them.

Now I want to show you something remarkable. Which of your two lists do you think has better things on it? For example, let's say in List A you put one million dollars (or one billion if you're really ambitious). And let's say you put "eyes" on List B.

Which would you rather have — eyes or one million dollars? Or even a billion dollars? Would you give up your legs for all that money?

What's the price tag on life itself?

Without exception, I have shown people that the list of what they *have* is much greater than the list of what they think they need in order to be happy. So if people already have a list of incredible blessings and are grumpy and dissatisfied, why should they believe that they would be happy if they had more things?

You might be surprised to hear that I've even had people with terrible problems acknowledge the pricelessness of their blessings.

The only ones who were reluctant to acknowledge how many wonderful things they had in their lives were people close to suicide. Being suicidal, by the way, comes from obsessive focus on what is lacking in one's life.

What can you learn from all this? It's wonderful to want new things, but you also have to take pleasure in the present moment. If your formula is "If I only had X, I'd be happy" — you'll *never* be happy. When you get X, you'll focus on not having Y. There's nothing wrong with wanting X and Y, but how about enjoying what you have in the meantime?

Boot Camp for Happiness

I remember the first time I ever taught a class on happiness. At one point, I asked students to make a list of some of the pleasures they'd had during the day. "Pick things you really felt strongly," I said.

Guess what was on the list. Things like awareness of God and helping an old lady cross the street.

"Come on, everybody," I said. "Those are things you *think* you're supposed to say. I want something you really *felt.*" One girl in the back of the class shyly raised her hand. "Does this count?" she asked. "I had a really great cup of coffee this morning."

"How did you feel when you drank it?"

"Terrific," she said.

"I sat in the sun and felt really good just before class," someone else said.

"I got a call from my sister a few hours ago," said a third.

Those are really good examples. When I ask for people to remember a moment of happiness, they think I am looking for something extraordinary or saintly. They pick giant things they think they should feel, but probably don't. And not too many giant things happen to us during the day. Life is composed of thousands and thousands of small moments.

The truth of the matter is that happiness is the natural state of a human being. Watch a baby for a few minutes. They don't seem to have too much trouble being happy.

To make the point, I bring trays of ice cream into seminars. Everyone's mood suddenly perks up and they're all smiles. The ice cream does the trick — it got them to forget their worries and focus on the goodness of life. Being happy should be a pleasure felt in the gut, not some abstract concept that stays in the mind.

Spend three days looking for your moments of happiness. Every time you feel a true shot of pleasure, notice it. You'll see that sometimes they are few and far between — not because there aren't many chances to feel them, but because you're worrying or focusing on what isn't going right.

Each moment can be filled with pleasure. If you were suddenly able to see or hear for the first time, you'd be filled with joy for at least a whole day.

Looking at a flower, seeing a friend walking toward you, enjoying something you're eating — all of these are moments of happiness.

People often ask me whether they should write down their happy moments and look at the list every day. The truth is, we don't have to hang onto the old ones. Every second is bringing new ones. Why look at a list of what happened yesterday?

Happiness is an attitude of noticing the good constantly coming our way. There's so much good coming every minute, there's no need to hang onto the past. We don't need to grasp onto a rope to prevent ourselves from drowning when we are standing on dry land.

The trick of it is to get into the habit of looking for good things, instead of griping all day about what's going wrong. I refer to this as a kind of boot camp. In boot camp, the army teaches a soldier how to instinctively do things he's never done before in his life, like marching or loading a weapon. We need to work at getting the same habits in happiness. We're often so consistently programmed to look for the bad or take our blessings for granted, that we become oblivious to all the interesting, pleasurable and good things around us.

Joy about the Future

Human beings live in time. I've found that it's not enough for people to just feel good about the present moment; they also need to feel optimistic about the future. This optimism is called "joy."

Joy means being excited about the future.

A person who feels that life is wonderful today but will be crummy next week will quickly get a case of the doldrums.

I took my kids on a trip to Disneyland a few years ago. They were so charged up the night before, they could hardly fall asleep.

Wouldn't it be great if we could live like this – so excited about the next day that we almost wish we didn't have to go to bed at night?

Joy gives us a feeling of power and energy.

There used to be a TV game show called "Supermarket Sweep." Contestants were given a shopping cart and let loose in a department store. They had two minutes to grab anything they wanted. Whoever's cart ended up stuffed with things worth the most money won all its contents. People dashed around the store like wild kangaroos.

This is one exaggerated example of the power of joy. (By the way, if you have joy about the future but no happiness in the present, you'll also be operating at half speed.)

People use a lot of methods to achieve joy. Some of them work great, but others are doomed to failure. Let's take a look at them.

- **Hysteria**

I like to use this one at seminars. Get a group of people in a room to start yelling, "Yippee! Hip-hip hooray!" Everyone starts laughing and the room becomes charged with energy. What they are feeling is, "Wow is this exciting. Something great is about to happen!" But will it?

The effects of joy like this never last more than a few minutes.

- **Illusion**

I have to be very careful how I explain this one or I'm going to get myself lynched. Professional sports are a very good example of this kind of joy. What happens when a baseball team wins the World Series? The city goes wild. Thousands of people pour into the streets chanting, "We're Number One, We're Number One."

In my sophomore year at college, the Detroit Tigers won the Series. Detroit was my hometown. The year before, the city had the worst race riot in American history.

I drove downtown with friends. Streamers were being thrown out of the windows of buildings, people were dancing on the roofs of their cars, strangers were hugging each other and flashing "V for victory" signs.

It was great fun. The reason I call it illusion is because if it's not turned into something meaningful, it dissipates quickly.

The joy came from feeling a kind of power— "Look at what we've just done. We can do anything if we work together." That's what joy is about. But just because 25 guys on a baseball team won the world championship doesn't mean that in the future *I'll* be able to accomplish much of anything.

That's why the optimism doesn't last.

- **A True Opportunity**
An example of this would be winning a million dollars in a lottery. The joy is that now you'll be able to do anything you want. But if you don't know what you want or you spin out of control, the opportunity fritters away.

I've read a number of stories about people who hit it big in a lottery. They buy boats, take vacations, get a new house and are besieged by opportunists. Before they know it, their life is worse than it was before. Hard to believe, but true.

It is a real opportunity, though.

- **The Real Thing**
People truly feel joy when they get married or have a child. Life becomes more meaningful. The joy comes from the anticipation of sharing a lifetime with someone you truly love. The future is bright. There will be strolls in the park, baby carriages, little league games, teenage years, a wedding.

It does contribute to a better life — the underlying reality is true.

- **The Essence of Joy**
This comes from feeling that you are doing something with your life that will give you meaning forever. It's what we humans are looking for. This kind of joy comes when, for example, you feel that you are growing in wisdom, making a difference in other people's lives or changing the world.

When people think they are just cogs in a machine or that their existence makes no difference to anyone, they feel a sense of sadness. "What's the point of it all?" they ask themselves.

In order to truly have a sense of joy, therefore, we need to feel that our relationships have permanence, and that our knowledge and good deeds have lasting value.

Many people feel — and I am one of them — that belief in God and in an afterlife are a helpful part of this feeling of optimism and joy.

Let's summarize the main points of this chapter: the Upper Soul (the third soul) lifts us into awareness and inspiration. The wings it uses to take off on its flight are happiness and joy. Happiness focuses us on the present moment. Joy is optimism about the future.

\\\\\\\\\\\\\\\\\\\\\\\\\\\\\\\

I know some people may be thinking that this is all very nice — but what about the fact that life has many reversals? Not everything is a bowl of cherries.

This is true. In the next chapter, we will discuss how to deal with the stresses and tragedies of life so that they don't shatter our spiritual awareness.

11 MAKING SUFFERING MEANINGFUL

> As each wave came, I dipped
> my head under and let it pass.
> *Talmud Bavli,*
> *Yevamos, 121a*

IN THE SUMMER OF 1997 I GOT THE PHONE CALL
that children with old parents dread receiving.

It was from my mother. "Tom," she said, "your father
fell out of bed and hurt himself. The doctors came and
put him in a nursing home."

"Are you ok, Mom?" Both of my parents were 85 years
old. The thought of my mother being alone in their apartment in Florida had me almost as worried as I was about
my father.

"Don't think about me," she said. "Just rush here as
fast as you can."

I caught the first flight down to Miami and by the
evening arrived at the nursing home. What greeted me

when I walked in was a shock to all my senses. The air was pervaded with the odor of human waste. People were sitting in wheelchairs in the hallways looking off into space. Cries were coming out of some of the rooms as I rushed down the hall in the direction that the nurses pointed me.

When I reached my father's room it was empty, so I ran to the nurses' station. "Do you know where George Meyer is?" I asked.

"You mean that nice, quiet man?" said one nurse. "He's in the television room down the hall."

There he was in a wheelchair, staring blankly at a television mounted on the wall. I went in front of the wheelchair and looked down at him.

"Dad! Dad! Do you recognize me?"

At first he didn't. Then a smile spread across his face. His lips quivered, "You've c-c-come. I-I-I knew you w-w-would."

I held him and started crying. "I love you Dad. Don't worry, I'll take care of you. I'm going to get you out of here and take you home with me." When I finally looked up, I saw a whole staff of workers looking at me with smiles. One of them, a male nurse, came over and said, "We usually don't see those kinds of feelings around here. It's nice to watch someone who loves his father so much."

What they didn't know was how many years I had kept that emotion in. I love both my parents dearly and appreciate all they have done for me. But I had never been able to show much open emotion to my father. It was a funny thing between us. He worked long hours when I was growing up and I didn't see too much of him. It created a distance between us. But now, misfortune and suffering were bringing us closer together.

This leads us to two important points to consider when we face reversals in life:

- *Often an event, which we think is terrible, leads us to important growth. Carbon is dirty and unattractive, but pressure on it can create a diamond.*

- *Even in our darkest moments when there seems to be absolutely no meaning to our suffering, we can transform tragedy into something positive.*

Rise to the Occasion

Sometimes I meet people whose goal seems to be avoiding pain. They run from anything that looks like it will hurt — personal relationships, responsibility, or the possibility of failure.

But they lose much more than they gain. Let's take a look at one example. Children can certainly cause pain. I'm a man, so I shouldn't talk about what it's like to give birth, but it sure doesn't look too easy. I've been at my wife's side during the birth of each of our children and thought, "If that were me, I would have taken a knockout pill as big as a hockey puck."

Bringing kids up can be difficult, too. First of all, there is crying in the middle of the night. It's one thing to get up at three in the morning to raid the refrigerator. It's quite another to drag yourself out of bed to change a smelly diaper.

Then as kids grow up, they go through some difficult experiences: a friend hurts their feelings, they don't make a baseball team, they struggle with their values and self-confidence, they start to rebel against authority. It's painful for them and for their parents.

But you know what? Outside of my wife, my children are the greatest pleasure in my life. I love bringing up my kids. The pain is *tiny* compared with the pleasure of one day's worth of coming home and having my kids run to the door to jump on Daddy.

Accept it. Pain isn't the enemy. Pain with no purpose is the enemy. We would take pain much better if we saw a great enough reason, and we admire people who do so.

When a human being is doing something meaningful, often he doesn't dwell on the suffering. I once met an elderly gentleman from the Netherlands. He told me about his experiences in the underground during World War II.

"That must have been frightening," I said. "You were hiding out from the Nazis. I'll bet it was the worst time in your life."

"Quite the opposite," he said. "It was the *best* time in my life." He saw my surprised look and smiled. "I know it's hard to understand. Before the war, I don't think I ever seriously helped another person. I was totally caught up in making money. Suddenly I found myself risking everything to save my country.

"Another thing — with all the horror and fear, at least I knew who I could trust. People from those days have remained my closest friends."

We see some of the positive qualities of suffering from the stories I just told. It can force us to acknowledge emotions we might otherwise have ignored, as with me toward my father. It can give someone heroic ability to overcome his or her own limits, as happened with the Dutch patriot.

People can endure suffering if they see a purpose; it can even increase their awareness and range of emotions.

The great eighteenth-century Kabbalist, Moshe Chaim Luzzatto, wrote that suffering has "the power to dispel the insensitivity in man, allowing him to become pure and clean."* He meant by this that it can break the stranglehold of the Animal Soul, thus giving the Spirit and Upper Soul a chance to exert themselves properly. Haven't most of us learned great lessons from times of trouble?

If a person becomes bitter, however, he will strengthen the Animal Soul even more. For example, I have unfortunately seen people hurt deeply by their choice of friends. Rather than learn to be more selective, they become angry at the world and decide not to trust anyone at all.

"This Too Is for the Good"

Sometimes events look awful on the surface, but really aren't. The Talmud tells a story about a sage named Rabbi Akiva who lived in the second century. He is mentioned as one of the great masters of Kabbala. He once came to a town and looked for an inn. There wasn't a single vacancy to be found, so he was forced to stay overnight in a field.

He had with him a candle, a rooster and a mule. Wind soon blew out the candle, a cat came and ate the rooster and a lion killed the mule.

In the middle of the night, foreign troops arrived and surrounded the town. If Rabbi Akiva had slept in the inn he would have been captured. Had the candle stayed lit or had his animals still been alive, he would have been detected.

---

*He wrote this in *The Way of God*, 2.2.5. Luzzatto (1707–1746) took the classic texts of Kabbala and laid them out in a systematic manner that the average person could understand. He spent most of his life in Italy and the Netherlands.

Life does have pain. Anyone who says otherwise is selling a fantasy. We don't have to stick our heads in the sand and pretend there are no difficulties. At the same time, it's helpful to remember that many apparent problems are not problems at all. We just don't see what's behind the shadows. Why get all upset right away, especially when worry clouds the mind, blurs judgment and drives the Upper Soul away?

Let me give an example of what I mean. Twenty years ago a friend of mine, Tuvia Ariel, told me one of the most powerful stories that I have ever heard. He had been working in a carpentry shop in Israel. Summers get very hot there, so they would often work in their T-shirts.

His boss was a burly refugee from Poland who had survived the concentration camp in Auschwitz.

One day Tuvia slipped and badly cut his leg. He left his job at the shop and got work as a cab driver, using his good foot on the pedals.

Shortly after he began his new job, he picked up a very fat man at the airport. The guy was an American citizen, but spoke with a thick, Eastern European accent.

"Right from the beginning I didn't like him," Tuvia told me. "He had very expensive clothing, too many gold rings on his fingers and an unpleasant way of speaking. He spit out orders like he owned me. After several rude comments while we were traveling, he noticed that I was bristling and on the verge of throwing him out of my cab. When we came to a red light, he leaned forward from the back of the car and said, 'You don't like me, huh? You think I'm obnoxious. How do you know what I've been through?' With that comment, he pushed up his suit sleeve and showed me a number tattooed on his arm.

"I stared at it in shock. 'Don't say anything more,' I blurted out. 'I'm taking you someplace, just trust me.'

"'What are you talking about?' he shouted as the car suddenly lurched in a different direction. 'Where are you going?'

"'Just trust me,' I repeated.

"I sped through the countryside until we came to the carpentry shop. I don't know why he didn't try to stop me, but he didn't.

"'Wait here a second,' I said. Then I went inside to get my old boss. There he was in a sweaty T-shirt with his arms exposed.

"'Tuvia! What? Where are we going?' I yanked him to the cab and pulled the foreigner out. They stared at each other for a few seconds, then started screaming and hugging like wild men.

"The numbers on their arm were different by one digit. They were brothers. I'd spent so much time working next to my boss, I knew the number on his arm by heart.

"I got in the car and drove off crying, leaving the two of them still hugging and weeping like babies.

"Neither of them would have ever known that the other was alive if I'd never hurt my foot."

\\

What a story! It teaches us that a bad accident can lead to something magnificent.

This attitude — looking for something good to come out of a bad situation — takes much determination to cultivate.

In the Talmud it is called, "This too is for the good." It means that in any situation, a person should try to be patient until he sees how events unfold. Certainly, he'll be much calmer than if he lives in irritation and fear after every seemingly negative twist in his life.

My attitude in unpleasant situations is that I must be getting something worthwhile. This is not pie-in-the-sky idealism. I believe it's the only way to survive and flourish as a human being.

Why get upset before we know the final outcome? Everything could work out and we would have drained our life energy by worrying needlessly.

Furthermore, we lose a lot of important lessons. I'll show you what I mean. I have a close friend, Michael Epstein, who has built up three large businesses. I asked him how he did it. "By failing a half-dozen times," he said.

"What are you talking about?"

"I had a nightclub and restaurant that I closed, and an oil-well that went dry. Some people would have dwelt on the failures and never pulled out of them. Failure is the price you pay for success. It's called 'seasoning' in life. Minimally you learn not to do it again. Do new stupid things, not old ones. And when you survive – people know that this is a guy that doesn't allow setbacks to get him down."

Michael is right. I've met a lot of extremely successful businessmen in my life. Most of them told me that one of the reasons they did so well was because they kept trying when most other people would have given up. That's an important point when it comes to misfortune and suffering. Try to learn something from it and move on – otherwise you'll get trapped in a vortex of negativity.

Most important of all, you could become bitter from the reversals in life. How many people do you know like this? Why become like them?

Here is a good attitude to have when events don't go your way:

- **Cultivate the trait of patience.** King Solomon used to wear a ring on which was inscribed, "This too will pass." Things usually are not as bad as they seem. And even if they are, endurance will help a lot more than depression.

- **Ask yourself, "Is there anything I can learn from this?"** It could be a lesson like "Don't talk to your wife that way, it is going to lead to a very bad day." Or "Choose your partner in business carefully." Or "Spend a few more dollars on a product so you don't end up with a piece of junk."

- **Look for new opportunities.**

- **Above all, don't let yourself become bitter.** An emotion like this is usually more destructive than any actual setback, because it causes you to focus on the negative in every event and person. What enjoyment can you get out of life if you're sucking on a lemon all day?

Our Darkest Moments

When terrible tragedy strikes, such as the death of someone we love, it becomes very difficult to keep a grip on the principles we have been discussing in this chapter.

Mourning for that person is necessary and good. It's important to acknowledge the relationship we had. If we don't go through a process of grief, emotions can stay knotted in us for a lifetime.

Yet we owe it to ourselves and the people we care about

to try to heal and regain optimism about life. This is easier said than done. In the final chapter of *Powers of the Soul,* I'm going to describe what Kabbala says happens to the soul after death. It will make the process of healing a lot easier.

Becoming involved in a positive activity can also help people pick themselves back up.

In the summer of 1997, I flew to New York to meet a man named Dan, whose twelve-year-old son had skied straight into a tree and died almost instantly. The accident had happened several years earlier. The story was horrible enough in itself, but what really tore at me was meeting this kind man. He told me that his emotions had simply gone numb. He functioned on a day-to-day level. He worked and took care of his remaining family. But inside he had no feelings whatsoever.

What struck me the most was that he didn't think he had the right to be happy. It would be like denying the importance of his son.

I felt that the best direction to go in was to get him involved in helping others. The Kabbalistic masters say that one of the best ways to bring back joy is by doing good deeds. Dan also had a hunger for reading spiritual books, which helped.

Nowadays he won't admit that he is doing better at all. But I can see that he is. He tutors kids with learning disabilities, and gives money to charity in his son's name.

Here is another example of a positive activity: a close friend of mine put together a memory album after her mother died. Then she made one for each of the grandchildren. She advises others to do this too, and says that it helped her get through the first difficult weeks.

There is no simple rule for everybody, of course.

Let me tell you about Zecharia Greinirman, a close friend of mine who died of cancer. This story of how he dealt with the disease is so remarkable that it's hard to believe, yet every word of it is true.

I first met him in Jerusalem, where I spent a few years teaching in a Rabbinical college. Zecharia was of medium height, but so stout and broad-shouldered that he seemed huge. All he ever wanted to do was help people. He was a teacher whose students loved him, a great husband and a father of four children. The oldest was under ten.

Then he got cancer and went to the U.S. for treatment. Months quickly passed. One afternoon, I was teaching a class when someone walked in the room and handed me a message — "Zecharia passed away this morning."

I had been so sure his illness wouldn't kill him that I hadn't even flown to Boston to visit him in the hospital. Now he was dead.

I was stunned and stopped my class. Zecharia and I had been so close. I introduced my future wife Sheryl to him before we were married, hoping he would say that she was great for me. (He did!)

I went home, told my wife the terrible news and went into my study. I sat silently for a few minutes. Suddenly I felt as if Zecharia were in the room, telling me to keep up my work and never stop teaching people.

"Wait a minute, Tom," I thought. "Let's not get out of control. It's only natural to think Zecharia is here. After all, he was your friend. But let's not start imagining things."

I turned on an extra lamp and sat back, but the feeling increased. I felt like I had to get outside for some air. Something was pushing me to go to the school where Zecharia and I had often taught together.

A short time later, I was sitting in the front row of the study hall. Students were scattered around the room. I sat there in silence. After a while, I looked at my watch – it was almost 10:00 p.m. I had been there for an hour.

Someone sat down next to me. "Excuse me," he said, "are you Tom Meyer?"

"Yes."

"Do you mind if I ask you a question?"

"Well, to tell you the truth…"

"Can you explain to me what the soul is? I know I'm being rather abrupt, but it's very important to me."

I suddenly felt weary. "I'd really rather not…"

"But I came all the way from Boston to speak with you."

"I'm sorry, but a very close friend of mine died today and I just don't feel like talking."

"What's his name?"

"You mean my friend?"

"Yes, what's his name?"

I thought the question odd. What difference could it make to him? "Zecharia Greinirman," I said.

"I was with him just a few days ago," he said. "I'm so sorry to hear that he died."

"What did you say? You were what?"

"I'm a radiologist at Brigham Hospital. I looked at his X-rays. I wasn't even his regular radiologist, but his doctor brought them to me."

"Why?" I asked.

"He wanted me to meet Zecharia. He was immensely influenced by his personality. The truth is, I don't believe in the soul. It doesn't exactly show up in a lab test."

He stared at me intensely for a moment. "Maybe I've

seen too many people die. Anyway, I looked at the X-rays. The cancer was in his pancreas – it was terrible, literally eating him up alive. 'He must be in absolute agony,' I said to his doctor.

"'That's the amazing thing,' his doctor told me. 'He never complains. He talks to the staff about the soul and God. When one of us told him he is going to die, he said that he would be dancing at his funeral. The guy's on fire.'

"'You mean he's crazy?'

"'You don't understand,' said his doctor. 'He's getting to *us*. I've started reading books on religion. He proved to one of the other doctors that God exists. I think he's got me convinced. You have to meet him. You'd better do it fast.'

"The next day, I went to Zecharia's room and introduced myself. He was extremely weak. I told him the doctors were saying that he could teach things about the soul. 'If you have the strength today, I'd like to hear what you have to say.'

"'Go to Jerusalem, to Tom Meyer,' he said. He shut his eyes, then opened them very slowly. 'I have no energy. He's the one for you.'

"I had one week's vacation coming, so I figured why not? I've never even been out of the United States. I flew here yesterday and now I've come to you. This is the address he gave me, this school."

I sat there in amazement. This man had been sent by Zecharia to speak with me, and now Zecharia was gone.

"Why did you think you would find me here at this late hour?" I asked.

"I just came to the address he gave me and someone pointed you out. Do you have time to sit with me?"

We talked half the night. At 3:00 a.m., we stood up to leave.

"It's a lot to assimilate," he said. "You are very convincing." We walked outside and went our separate ways.

In the morning I told Sheryl what had happened. She wasn't even surprised.

"That's Zecharia for you," she said. "The cancer got to his body but it didn't get to him."

And that's the point. The Animal Soul wants to run the show and overwhelm the higher souls even in the best of times. In our worst moments, it has all the advantages. "Why go on?" it says. "Why look for meaning? Why be happy? What difference does it make anyway?"

But the higher souls will never fully accept this. The Spirit wants to use free will properly. The Upper Soul wants to provide wisdom and burst through the barriers into spiritual consciousness. Why deprive ourselves of so much pleasure?

There is no peace in giving up. For every reason that I've given in this chapter — even in your worst moments don't give up! Not everyone can be a Zecharia, happy and uncynical to the end. Most of us can be a Dan — giving to other people to feel the value of life.

And now, having understood how to overcome life's reversals or at least to give it a heck of a good battle, we are ready to continue our journey. In the next chapter, we'll see how to help the Upper Soul shine through in all its glory.

WISDOM AND ENLIGHTENMENT

> The man who changes himself externally, but not internally, is like the midget who woke up in the middle of the night and cried out, "I've grown, I've grown!" Never before did he stretch from one end of the bed to the other. However, when he put on the light he saw his error. Instead of sleeping lengthwise, he was lying across the width.
>
> *The Alter Rebbi from Nevardok*

A FRIEND OF MINE ONCE WENT TO A PLAY ON Broadway that succeeded in getting the audience to feel like they were attending a real wedding. The actors moved from room to room and the audience followed them. My friend went into one room and watched the future in-laws argue, and entered another room and met the bride and groom. Then came the wedding itself followed by the celebrations. When the show was over, he felt like he had actually been to a joyous event.

It's an interesting idea for a play, and it's also true about all of life: it takes place on a stage of constantly revolving sets. Most of the time, we forget this. We become so obsessed with the swirling dance of events that we lose our separateness from them.

For the Upper Soul to pour its wisdom into us, we have to open ourselves to its influence. If we flood our minds with life's continuous dramas, we lock out the Upper Soul. (If you don't let someone get past the front porch of your house, how much of a relationship are you going to have?)

Years ago I spoke in numerous homes across Russia. I would go to a house, twenty people would show up and we would talk about some of the ideas we're discussing in this book.

I flew back to New York. When I walked down the streets of the city, I was startled at the contrast between Russians and Americans. (In those days, the average Russian led a very austere, uncomplicated life.) People looked absolutely distracted, as if they were listening to two radio stations at the same time.

More and more things crowd our attention today. We need to find good ways to nourish our spiritual lives. One way to do this is to set ten minutes aside each day for what I call a "Soul Break." It's important for the soul, just like setting aside time to eat is important for the body.

Ten minutes is not a lot of time, yet people often tell me that they don't have it. Imagine what it was like to live two hundred years ago. If you wanted clean clothes, you drew water from a well and spent hours doing laundry by hand. Now all you have to do is throw everything into a washing machine and press a button. Do you think we have a lot more time? No way. The day gets filled up immediately because nature abhors a vacuum.

And how much time would you have spent taking care of your horse? You had to feed and clean it, not to mention dealing with what was left on the floor of the stable.

Now we have cars. We also have dryers, microwaves, computers – the list goes on and on. Yet we have less time than ever before!

This teaches us an important lesson. The Animal Soul will never let us think clearly unless we become the boss of our own lives. This means that we must help the Upper Soul give direction and awareness to the other two souls.

The Animal Soul knows that if you take a ten-minute Soul Break every day, your life will change forever. It's not so sure that it wants that to happen. All change frightens the Animal Soul because it wants to be comfortable. It doesn't realize, unless taught, the pleasures that await it.

A great time to take ten minutes is just before breakfast. You probably never skip having a bite to eat in the morning. Why not take care of your soul, too?

What should you do during your Soul Break?

I've arranged thirty-one topics for you to reflect on, one for each day of the month. (In a shorter month like February, you would only do the first twenty eight, then go back to number one on March 1.)

You don't have to wait until the first of the month to start. If you begin on August 7th, for example, jump to topic seven and continue from there.

When you work on these ideas, the light of the Upper Soul will begin to burst forth and its radiance will surround you. With each monthly repetition, you will see hidden meanings and spiritual disciplines.

Your Monthly Spiritual Calendar

1.

Think of how you have been given the opportunity to experience the beauty of life.

Is there any gift greater than life itself? We have been told that we are a collection of molecules with no soul, a speck of dust in the cosmos. What a destructive, limiting idea!

For ten minutes feel the exhilaration of being a soul with the entire universe before you. You can learn anything you want and grow in any way you want.

Do you remember being a child and feeling happy as you ran free? Recapture that unhindered feeling of pleasure in the adventure of life.

2.

Think of the wonderful gift you have been given in the form of a body.

At the beginning of your existence, you were provided with a fortress — your mother's body — to shelter you from the world. Food was provided for you. Then you emerged outside where oxygen was ready for your first breath. You continued to grow until reaching adulthood. Think of all the parts of the body that help you. You have hands for giving and receiving, feet for walking, eyes for seeing, nostrils for smelling, the mouth for eating, teeth for chewing, the stomach for digesting and tubes for removing wastes. The heart is a natural engine that keeps us alive. The brain is the seat of the Upper Soul. If you lacked eyes or hands and suddenly received them, imagine how happy you would be!

Feel wonder and gratitude for these gifts. You'll be a happier person.

3.

Consider the powers of the mind — memory, imagination, perception and reason — and the advantages they give you.

Take memory, for example: What would your condition be if you couldn't remember your name, where you live or something as complex as how to drive a car? What if you forgot what you had seen and heard throughout life? You would have no memories of people you love. You would lose most of the qualities that make up a human being. Feel thankful in your soul that these gifts have been given to you.

4.

Involve your body and soul together in meaningful activities

Many people think that in order to live a truly spiritual life, they would have to scorn money, possessions and the pleasures of this world. They would have to neglect their body. It's not true at all. Most people would become utterly depressed living like that. They should instead hold fast to an awareness of the importance of the soul, yet not ignore the body or the physical world.

The best advice is to keep to the middle of the road: enjoy physical pleasure, but be careful not to drown in a sea of lusts.

According to Kabbala, the soul is eternal. True, the body returns to the dust, but in the meantime it is the soul's valuable companion. The two are temporarily "married" and they should do things as a team.

Think of one physical activity that you are going to do, and come up with a way to add a spiritual component to it. One example would be to listen to a meaningful tape while jogging. Another would be to take someone you love out to dinner at a good restaurant, as a way to spend special time together.

5.

Don't be satisfied with conclusions you reached earlier in life about deep subjects such as the existence of God, life after death and the value of prayer.

At what age did you reach your conclusions? Based on what information? For the stronger the intellect becomes in a human being, the clearer he can understand deep themes. Think about these subjects as if you were seeing them for the first time. Come to your own conclusions. Don't let the Animal Soul trick you into thinking that your perception hasn't increased over the years.

6.

Pinpoint your worst habit.

The Animal Soul uses different strategies when it wants to overwhelm the higher souls. For some people it is obsession with money, for others it is sitting passively in front of a television set day after day.

Do one action in the next day to counteract your worst habit. Here's an example: if it is obsession with work, leave early one afternoon and take someone you love out to a restaurant.

7.

Are your public and private lives consistent?

Some people are supportive and kind in their home, but difficult to get along with in the workplace or socially. Others act with dignity and kindness in public, but are a scourge in their own home.

Try to act with generosity both publicly and in the privacy of your home. Think of an inconsistency in these two domains and do one action to improve your behavior.

8.

Pray.

Ask for something from God. People sometimes think that they have no right to bother God with what might seem like a petty request.

An old story helps put this into perspective. Once there was a man who was driving his wagon to the city. He saw a fellow standing on the side of the road with a heavy pack on his back. The driver stopped the horse and asked the man if he'd like a ride. The fellow pulled himself up and sat down. When the horse started forward again, the driver noticed that the man still had the pack on his back.

"Why don't you put that in the back of the wagon?" he asked.

"You have already been so kind to me," said the traveler. "How can I possibly ask you to carry my pack, too?"

This story is meant to teach us that it's not a burden on God when we ask for help. He is there for the big things, and the little things, too.

9.

Is your life more about being a better person, or about getting immediate gratification?

Consider the portion of life that has passed. Have you mostly occupied yourself with the goals of your higher souls, which want wisdom and good deeds, or of your Animal Soul?

Imagine that you are a stockbroker whose entire account is with one rich man. He tells you to carefully watch his money and that he will come back at the end of a year. Wouldn't you closely monitor the investments to know how they are doing?

Similarly, don't suddenly be taken by surprise after years have passed. If you haven't monitored your life up to now, do so from now on. Each day is a page — make sure your book has the story you want.

10.

Who are your friends and why?

Rabbeinu Yonah of Gerona (1180?–1263) was a great sage who lived in Spain. He wrote that a good friend should have three qualities:

- He wants to grow as a person.
- He wants to do the right thing. He'll try to stop you when you're behaving destructively.
- You can turn to him for help and trust him with your secrets.

Do your friends have these qualities?

The Talmud says that an unknown type of bird once flew into a city. Students came to their rabbi and asked whether it was permitted to eat it. (Birds of prey such as eagles and hawks, for example, are off limits according to the dietary laws of Judaism. Eating them weakens the power of the higher souls.)

"Observe which species of birds it seeks for company," he replied. "You will have your answer."

This, of course, is the idea that "birds of a feather flock together." Friends influence us. If they care about spiritual growth, so will we. If they don't, with whom will we share our feelings?

11.

Recall times when you had the feeling of awe.

The easiest way to get it is through an aesthetic experience. When we are out in nature or see children playing happily, we feel the beauty of the world. This is a quiet type of awe. For a moment we are transfixed out of our daily routine. There is also an overpowering type of awe as, for example, when we see snow-capped mountains soaring into the sky or a great thunderstorm. It's an extremely inspiring emotion and worth pursuing.

Act as if you are seeing your surroundings after a long absence. Notice the details: people, grass, trees, animals and insects. Look at the sky. Don't only focus on the physical beauty; also experience the genius and unity that infuses everything.

If rain falls on a garden, the water takes on the hue of each flower. No one would ever think that a red liquid fell on the roses and a white liquid landed on the lilies. All of the water in the garden is of the same composition and from the same source. The same is true of the wisdom imbuing all of nature — it is all from one source, though it appears in different forms.

12.

Pack your bags carefully for the next world.

When you are going on a long trip or vacation, you probably think a lot about what to bring. Think about what accomplishments you want to take with you when you embark on the journey from this world – a journey from which there is no escape and which can come at any moment.

13.

Consider the superiority of the soul to the body.

Even in the case of a beautiful woman or handsome man, if spiritual refinements are lacking, their looks won't remain important for long. That's why it's so dangerous to marry someone for physical attraction alone – the excitement fades pretty quickly. As important as the body is, increase your attention to the condition of your soul. The body wears down and ages, but the soul can become stronger.

It may seem that the soul declines when a person becomes senile or develops Alzheimer's, but this too is due to the frailties of the body, in this case the brain.

If we consider the body supreme, we will never put in effort to achieve wisdom. We will favor appearance over substance and will panic as the body begins to age.

14.

What is your most positive character trait? What is your weakest one?

Take pleasure in your strengths and don't get down on yourself for faults, because the Animal Soul won't learn from you if you insult it.

15.

What was your past day like?

Do you spend more time doing what is important to you or chasing distractions? Decide on one small change that will improve your ability to focus your day.

16.

Which trait do you wish to possess the most?

Plan one action that you'll do in the next twenty-four hours to help acquire it.

17.

Do you enjoy seeing other people succeed? Do you enjoy helping them?

Kabbala tells us that the world was created with ten traits, the greatest of which is pure kindness. Apply this trait to your relationships with people. It's an especially great way to strengthen the higher souls over the Animal Soul.

I can illustrate this with an example. Imagine that you are on a sports team with twenty-five players. If the desire of the players is the success of the whole team, they will get the best results. But if they are divided and each one solely tries to further his own interests, they'll soon begin to grumble. Quarreling will break out. Not only won't they help each other, they'll even be jealous of each other's success. Eventually the team will self-destruct, even if they were champions the year before.

So it is in life. People can cooperate so that the world yields much for everyone, or they can want more than their proper share. Many will end up mourning over their lot in life even if they have great wealth.

Be happy to help others improve their talents and enjoy their lives. Help one person with this in mind during the day.

18.

What is the most important lesson you have learned in life?

Think about it until you are clear, then tell it to one person. Make sure that it is not cynical. A cynic never believes in the sincere, idealistic motives of other people and generally has a low opinion of everything. Oscar Wilde, a nineteenth century British author, wrote that a cynic "knows the price of everything and the value of nothing."

19.

Take care of your body.

If a friend lent you his car, wouldn't you take care of it? Wouldn't you put in the proper oil and gas? The body has also been lent to you. Treat it with care. If you neglect the body, you'll end up weakening it and burdening the soul.

Ask yourself: Is the condition of your body helping or hurting you? What one thing can you do in the next day to improve it?

20.

Decide to investigate the wonders of the universe, from the largest stars to the smallest microorganisms.

Read science articles for the layman and subscribe to magazines about nature. Notice the world in motion around you – sun, moon and stars; sunrise and sunset; streams and seas, clouds and rain.

A word for bush in Hebrew is *si'ach,* which is also the word for "conversation," because nature is always talking to us, even if it is only a plant.

Every animal teaches us some important character trait, such as loyalty or humility. Don't neglect studying the phenomena of nature, for it will widen your intellect and add to your awe of creation.

21.

Do good deeds for other people for the right motives.

Watch how people behave when it comes to relationships: if someone feels that his friend isn't sincere in his friendship or is helping him for an ulterior motive, he becomes distrustful or hurt.

How can we allow an attitude in ourselves that would upset us in others?

Do one favor for someone in the next day, whose sole motive is to do good.

22.

How do you react when mishaps occur?

They can happen to your body, property, plans or daily affairs. There are three ways of dealing with a problem:

- Learn from it and try to solve it.
- Complain.
- Don't deal with it.

In other words, you can solve, gripe or ignore. We are combinations of all three. Pick one problem you will face in the next day that you would normally get upset about, and work on solving it without complaint.

23.

Be grateful to people who help you.

Imagine if when you were a baby, your parents had abandoned you on the open road. A man passing by saw you, felt pity and brought you to his home. He took responsibility for you until you grew up and paid for your education. How grateful you would be!

Well, how did we make it to where we are? People must have helped along the way. Do we feel grateful to them? Some people don't like to feel the emotion of gratitude, because they think that they did everything on their own, or they're worried about being obligated. They are truly hurting themselves. Gratitude brings a bonus — the realization that we have been given many gifts and a lot of help. Then we don't feel the world has held back its good things from us.

Think of the names of three people who helped you in an important way in the past year.

24.

Consider the portion of your life that has passed.

What have been your most important accomplishments? Write them down and enjoy them.

25.

Don't talk against other people.

Don't mention their failings or discredit them. If you think someone has a weakness, talk to him directly or write him a note, even anonymously. If you need advice or help against someone who is harassing you, speak to a responsible person who won't begin spreading tales. Stay away from a gossip because you will be his next victim. Gossip divides people and increases hate. Help people see their value, don't destroy it.

Kabbala teaches that when a person separates from his body at death, he will learn that some of his accomplishments have been taken away and given to others. This was done as compensation for the victims of his words.

26.

Do you use a portion of your money to do good deeds?

None of our possessions remain with us forever. Shrouds have no pockets, because the dead don't need them. Therefore, be sure that you use your money to take care of your soul as well as your body.

Pick one good cause that you believe in, and make a donation to it of whatever amount you consider right.

27.

Be open to receiving influences from the higher souls.

Light a candle and stare at it. The Animal Soul clings to the body like the dark light at the bottom of the candle flame clings to the wick. The brighter light is above it. When we feel joy, we connect to the higher souls, which are like the bright part of the candle's flame. Darkness departs and the body itself feels lighter.

Focus for a moment on the agitation you have when you're worried or angry, as opposed to when you feel love or beauty. In the same way, if you shake the candle, the bright part of the flame mixes with the dark tail. The flame may even become extinguished.

Anger and worry do to the lower souls what shaking a candle does to the flame. Conquer these negative emotions and you will experience more spirituality during the day.

28.

Consider the length of stay on Earth for someone who reaches even a very old age.

How quickly time passes! The years fall away like autumn leaves. Strengthen your determination to meet your spiritual goals rather than let life slip away.

29.

Avoid arrogance like a disease.

Nothing causes the Upper Soul to flee more quickly than this trait. An arrogant person thinks he reaches great heights, but his Animal Soul drags him deep into the sea of illusions like a boulder tied to the neck. On the other hand, take pleasure in your accomplishments. This will give you the confidence and energy to do much more.

For example, enjoy your house. But don't think you are better than someone with a smaller one.

30.

Treasure your Upper Soul.

The Spirit makes us human because it has free will. The Upper Soul is even greater, for it puts us in touch with God. It desires the immense pleasure of spiritual consciousness. No blemish can damage it, because it departs when a person is destructive. Treasure its company and you will lift your entire being into the glow of Eternity.

31.

Never think that you have finished growing.

A billion Einsteins could barely touch the surface of what the soul can know.

Now that you have finished all thirty-one topics, begin them again.

Drink from the River

When a person masters these thirty-one topics, a wonderful awareness enters him. He discovers the soul's very essence. He acts with a pure heart, his understanding is illuminated and he sees the road to happiness. He acquires a new celestial power that he didn't know existed and begins to see profound secrets.

Imagine that an archeologist dug up an ancient marble statue that was encrusted with lime. He applied many chemicals to it and polished it for a long time. Finally, its luster returned. He was astonished at its wondrous beauty. The statue in this analogy represents the soul. The chemicals represent the thirty-one topics that I have set out above. When you turn them over in your mind, their light will burst forth and surround you. If you repeat the cycle monthly, hidden meanings will occur to you that you didn't think of at first.

The wisdom that comes from the Upper Soul is like a great river whose waters never stop flowing. We can endlessly drink from it. Many people, unfortunately, experience only the slightest effect of the Upper Soul on their conscious thoughts, because they haven't developed their ability to receive from it. The thirty-one topics will change this.

Even if you aren't yet familiar with its power, the Upper Soul can effect your mind in unusual ways. The Talmud says, "Even though a person does not see, his destiny sees." This means that we sometimes get flashes of intuition, though a complete picture is not transmitted to the mind. Did you ever think about someone you hadn't seen for a while, when suddenly the phone rang and

…guess who it was? Or did you worry for no reason about a family member and then find out he was having problems at that very time? These illuminations may have come from the Upper Soul, which imparts wisdom and spiritual consciousness, and can even connect us with souls whose physical bodies are thousands of miles away.

Now it is time, dear reader, to move on with our journey. Carrying with us the ideas that we have learned so far, we are ready to discover the fourth soul.

THE FOURTH SOUL AND THE
ROOT OF YOUR IDENTITY

This above all: To thine own self
be true.
William Shakespeare,
Hamlet, I.iii

THE FIRST THREE SOULS REST IN DIFFERENT PARTS
of the body (the liver, heart and brain). The light of the
fourth soul, however, is so strong that it is not contained
in the body.

The fourth soul, called the *Chaya* in Hebrew, or *Life
Source*, is the root of the other souls. It gives life to them,
but its actions are too sublime to be felt directly.

What do I mean when I say it is the root of the other
souls? This is somewhat comparable to a tree whose roots,
though buried deep underground, are connected to the
rest of the tree and nourish all its parts. The same is true
of the fourth soul. It exists in a world that is not directly
experienced by us as long as we are in the physical world.
Yet it gives life to the first three souls.

Know Your Root

The Life Source is the root of the first three souls in another important way. People often try to trace their genealogies nowadays. What are they searching for? I believe they are searching for information that will help them understand themselves better.

The greatness of this need was brought home to me in 1997 when I visited Poland with my eldest son. We were staying in a hotel in Warsaw. My son, who was thirteen years old at the time, pulled me into the lobby one morning. "Dad," he said, "I want you to meet someone." He brought me to a blond woman who was sitting with an old man. "Could you please tell my father your story?" said my son. "I think it's incredibly interesting!"

She was eager to talk. "Yesterday was the most important day of my life," she said.

It seemed perfectly natural to listen to this animated woman as she told me her life story, though I knew her less than a minute. I sat down with my son, who was happy to hear her repeat it.

"I'm from Los Angeles, but I was born here in Warsaw," she began. "During World War II, the Nazis conquered Poland. My father and mother took me to an orphanage run by nuns and left me there. Although my parents were Jewish, they felt I would be safe. During a major roundup in the Jewish ghetto, the Nazis chased my father into a building. He ran up the stairs and ducked into an open apartment. He could hear soldiers coming up the stairs behind him."

At this point her father, who was the old man sitting next to her, broke into the story.

"I thought I might as well jump out to the street. If they got me they would probably kill me anyway. I preferred to take my chances, so I ran headlong toward a large open window and leaped through. I landed on a pile of mattresses and wasn't even scratched! Then I made my way out of the ghetto into the non-Jewish side of Warsaw. I managed to get false papers and hide for the rest of the war. After the war was over I went back to the orphanage to get my daughter."

His daughter continued the story. "I remember my father taking me from the orphanage. I was only four years old at the time and didn't remember his face. There was no woman with him. Somehow I knew my mother must be dead. A short time later we managed to come to America and ended up in Los Angeles. For years and years I did not believe this was really my father. Where was the proof? Why should I have believed him?

"Seven years ago I came back to Warsaw looking for the orphanage. My father didn't remember the name or even where it was. All the streets were different. What had been rubble after the war was now a built-up city. I walked through the streets but couldn't find anything to jog my memory.

"A few weeks ago I convinced my father to return to Warsaw for the first time in over fifty years. Two days ago, which was the morning after we arrived, I woke up very early. My father was still asleep and I was restless, so I went out walking alone. As I went down one old narrow street, I suddenly felt that I had been there before. I let my instincts lead me until I came to a large building. I went inside. The sounds and smells seemed familiar. There were little children running around and nuns walking down the halls.

"One of the nuns came up to me. 'Can I help you?' she asked. I told her my story. 'I wasn't here during the war,' said the nun, 'but the Mother Superior who ran this place is still alive. She lives in an old age home and her memory is as clear as a bell. Come back tomorrow and I will take you there.'

"Yesterday morning I took my father to the orphanage. He didn't really remember it. The nun was waiting for us and took us to the old age home. When we entered the Mother Superior's room, she sat up in her chair and smiled at us. 'I remember you,' she said, pointing to my father. 'You're the man who brought his little daughter to us during the war and came to get her afterwards.'

"My heart started beating like mad. 'How do you know it's the same man?' I said. 'More than fifty years have passed!'

"My father burst out laughing. 'Maybe I haven't aged so much,' he said.

"'Your face is much the same,' the Mother Superior said to him. 'And I can tell you exactly what you were wearing when you came to get your daughter.' She proceeded to describe a pair of shiny leather boots and a cap that I remember quite well.

"I was ecstatic. 'Now I know that he is really my father!'" I cried out.

I sat on the edge of my seat listening to this woman's story. She looked at me with one of the biggest smiles I've ever seen. "Last night was the first really good night's sleep I've had since I was a child," she said. "Now I'm truly certain of my roots."

We want to know our roots because we want to know who we really are. The woman from Los Angeles was overjoyed to be certain that this man was her father, because it told her something important about herself.

We are used to thinking of roots and genealogies in terms of tracing the source of our physical body. But it is also possible to think about the root of our soul in the spiritual world. The fourth soul – the Life Source – is this root.

What do we mean when we talk about the Life Source in this deep, esoteric way?

The Ten Primary Forces

In order to explain this, I'm going to introduce some new concepts.

Kabbala teaches that ten Divine emanations form the basis of Creation. They are the most elementary forces of existence. Although they are not themselves physical, they spawn the dimensions of space and time. They also give birth to the spiritual dimension, which includes the soul.

Each of these ten emanations is called a *Sefira* in Hebrew. The word literally means "counting" or "numeration." Sometimes each one is called a "Koach," which means "Force." I've chosen to use the word Force because it is easier to understand.

Everything in existence has its origin in the Forces. Their names are:

	Hebrew	*English*
1	Keter	Crown
2	Chachma	Wisdom
3	Bina	Understanding
4	Chesed	Lovingkindness
5	Gevurah	Strength
6	Tiferet	Beauty

7	Netzach	Victory
8	Hode	Splendor
9	Yesod	Foundation
10	Malchut	Kingship

The ten Forces are the roots of existence. By the time we have an actual physical object in front of us, like a rose bush or a squirrel, the Forces aren't recognizable at all. Just as a squirrel has invisible physical forces working in it (such as electromagnetism, and the strong and weak forces), so too invisible spiritual forces are at work bringing the squirrel into existence and maintaining it.

As you can see, the Forces have the same names as human traits. That is because they behave similarly. The beginning Forces — Crown, Wisdom and Understanding — are called "the Forces of thought."

Crown is the trait of Will. Will is the beginning of any action. Nothing happens if some aspect of Crown does not initiate it. It gets its name from the fact that, just as a king's crown rests on his head, so too Crown is above the other Forces.

A human being's behavior is similar: no process is ever set in motion unless it is desired and willed.

The second Force is Wisdom. After a person desires something, the beginning of thought flashes in him. For example, first someone desires a place to live, than a general picture of a house is drawn in his mind. At this stage only a broad idea exists, whose details remain mostly hidden.

The next Force is Understanding. In this stage, a person uses his intellect to analyze the image that appeared in his mind. He labors to build it into a detailed plan. (The Hebrew word for understanding, *"bina"* is related to the word *"boneh"* which means to build). He had first imagined a house with huge balconies, but then realizes no such thing exists in the neighborhood and they'll stick out like an igloo in Florida. He wants the bedrooms on the second floor. The office will be wood-paneled. Double oak doors and large picture windows add elegance to the future dwelling. He decides on a circular driveway and wants a set of swings in the backyard.

The next three Forces — Lovingkindness, Strength and Beauty — are those of emotion. The Force of Lovingkindness is the power of unrestrained giving, regardless of the capacity of an object to receive. It can be compared to light in that it has no bounds. If the Force of Lovingkindness rules, the desire to spend on the house grows without restraint. The best of everything will be purchased.

The fifth Force is Strength (sometimes called "Justice"). It has the power to restrict the influence of Lovingkindness. If the size of an object weren't restricted, for example, it would go on forever and never get its form. Strength here is meant in the sense of holding back and providing laws that give borders. Limiting the power of Lovingkindness is not negative; the Force of Strength withholds from an object what it cannot absorb. When our homebuilder realizes the soaring cost of the house and its furnishings, he controls his passion and settles for something within his means.

The sixth Force is Beauty. It blends the previous two emotions, Lovingkindness and Strength, so that they achieve harmony. In pure Lovingkindness, one would like to pour all his money into the house he is building. It could bankrupt him and absorb all his time. With pure Strength, he would want to build only what is necessary, making the house feel cold and austere. Beauty blends these two extremes. If done in proper measure, a balanced emotional approach will be reached and the house will become a home.

The next three are Victory, Splendor and Foundation. They are a transition from emotions into action. Now our builder is ready to put up his house. Victory is the trait of dominance and assertion. Its tendency is to translate the emotions of the previous Forces without limitation on time or amount. It gives the optimum possible. It's the equivalent to putting a foot on the gas.

The eighth Force, Splendor, limits the transmission of the other Forces. It means giving the optimum possible according to the capacity of the receiver. What if the ground is too soft to bear the weight of stone? He will have to use lighter material. It's like putting a foot on the brakes. Every real estate developer knows that adjustments occur between planning and implementation. (Hence the name "Splendor" — intelligent limitations can produce splendid results.)

The ninth Force, Foundation, is the final decision-maker. It mediates all the influences of the previous Forces.

Kingship is the final Force. It receives and then passes on all the abundance of the other Forces to created things. The more Kingship receives, the more it gives. Now the house will be completed (or, in the case of Creation of the world, the rock, plant or dog will now exist and be sustained). What began as Crown (the first Force, which is the power of Will) ends as Kingship, in which the spiritual forces are actualized in a physical creation. This is like a human king, who uses all his resources to properly run his realm.

In summary, in the process of Creation we find the following stages:

- **desire**
- **planning**
- **action**
- **completion**

Root of the Soul

What does all this have to do with the root of our soul?

The Forces are the roots of everything in existence. They are a blend of qualities that, put together, determine the nature of an object: its color, texture and other physical properties. The way the Forces combine to form the root of gold differs from the way they combine to form the root of tin.

This is also true of living creatures. A lion has different spiritual roots than a giraffe.

The Forces are also the root of the human soul and determine the innate character of every single person. They give us our differing qualities as thinkers, feelers and doers. Not only is every person's face different, the root of his soul is different too.

The Forces can combine in an almost infinite number of ways. When you were a child, you probably played with a kaleidoscope. As you turned it, the little colored stones lined up differently each time to form a new image. In a way, the Forces behave similarly. Although there are only ten of them, each one actually has subunits consisting of all the other Forces. Take Crown for example: this first Force has all ten Forces in it. There is Crown of Crown, Understanding of Crown, Wisdom of Crown, etc. Each of these subunits has another ten subunits, and so on. The possible combinations produce billions of variations.

Species have similar roots, therefore, but the differences in the subunits create wide-ranging individuality.

The fourth soul — the Life Source — contains the full power of all ten Forces and their subunits. If a person were able to totally link up with his Life Source, the immense spiritual power of all ten Forces would be within his grasp. The light of the Life Source is so powerful, however, that the human body can only contain it if a person exists on an extraordinarily high spiritual level. Theoretically, if a person lived a life of absolute perfection he would be able to draw the fourth soul into his body. Under such conditions, the Life Source's full power would be available to him.

If he lets the Animal Soul rule, however, the Life Source eludes him. It will not rest within the body at all. Instead, it remains in the spiritual realm – the root of his soul, yet not united with it.

If the Life Source would enter the body, we would become extraordinary thinkers, feelers and doers beyond our wildest dreams. Every one of us would move history. Because we are not connected with the full power of the fourth soul, however, each of us is inclined by nature toward one of these three areas.

Kabbala teaches that the form of the human body reflects these ten Forces:

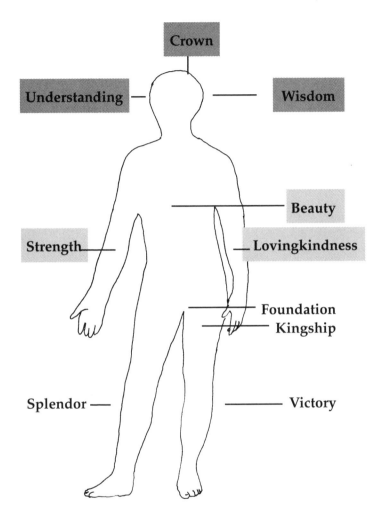

The body is divided into three parts — the head, the torso and the legs. The skull, which surrounds the brain, corresponds to the Force of Crown. The right brain and left brain correspond to the Forces of Wisdom and Understanding.

The middle part of the body is the area of the heart. In this area, the right hand corresponds to Lovingkindness, the left hand to Strength and the torso to Beauty. In the lower part of the body, the right leg corresponds to Victory, the left to Splendor, and the sexual organ to Foundation and Kingship.

These three divisions of the Forces correspond to three personality types. Some people are "head-oriented." They love ideas and are always analyzing something – themselves, others or concepts. I call them Thinkers. Some are "heart- oriented" people. They like to be with others and help them. These I call Feelers. And some people are task-oriented. They love responsibility and getting a job done. They have an intense drive to do the right thing. I call them Doers.

We accommodate aspects of all three types in ourselves. We are by nature, however, most comfortable with one. Let's now look at these three personalities in depth.

The Thinker

We'll begin with the Thinker. What kind of person is he?

The Thinker's deepest spiritual drive is for truth and understanding. He is always talking about ideas – on religion, politics, movies, art and philosophy – you name it.

Even sports. I was once playing on the same touch-football team with a friend of mind named Mike. Mike is a bit of an extremist. He kept trying to explain why we should go into a complicated zone defense. A few players listened for a moment, then gave up. "Give me a break," one of them said. "It's touch football, not astrophysics." Granted, Mike is a bit over the edge, but you get the point:

if a thinker doesn't figure out how to explain his ideas in concrete terms, he loses the Feelers and Doers.

A Thinker enjoys analyzing people and understanding them. He wants to know what makes them tick.

When Thinkers learn how to talk to Doers and Feelers, they make great management consultants, psychologists and stock market analysts. The common denominator of these jobs is that they require the ability to pick out patterns and come up with strategies and solutions. They often require a lot of reading. Thinkers have the patience to do this. But they have to learn how to explain themselves on other people's levels.

A Thinker who masters this ability has it made. He can take the most abstract material and bring it down to earth. He'll show *anybody* how to use that new computer program. Doers and Feelers usually don't want to know the theories. "Permutations shmurmutations" they say. "Just tell me how to use the blasted thing."

I have a friend named David who gets into discussions about religion that drive Feelers and Doers crazy. To Feelers, the ideas are too abstract unless they involve relationships and people. To Doers, they are spacey unless they have practical applications.

Let me give an example. I once watched David spend an hour trying to prove to a Doer that God exists.

Finally the Doer said, "Look, what difference does it make? I try to be a good person whether or not there is a God."

"What difference does it make?" David was stunned. "If there is no God, the world is nothing but billions of randomly swirling molecules. There would be no such thing as right and wrong."

The other person didn't know what David was talking about. They were at cross-purposes. Talking abstract philosophical ideas was a waste of time to the fellow, like sitting on a flagpole and puffing on a hookah pipe. Amusing to watch for a few minutes, but spacey unless relevant in practical terms.

David loves talking about his theories. He approaches the world through concepts that he constantly tries to improve. He is often absorbed in figuring out the meaning of events, trying to weave them into a systematic view of life. Lack of clarity annoys and even depresses him.

Here is another interesting facet of David's character: he has a constant drive toward self-awareness, endlessly analyzing his actions and motives.

When the Animal Soul gets hold of the Thinker, he is easily distracted. If he has a project, it never ends — he tinkers with it forever, reading more and more and redoing it until it's perfect. To the Feeler and Doer, he's lost in abstract trivia. To the Thinker, the other types are intellectually sloppy at best and dishonest at worst.

Books easily capture him. "Capture" is the right word: he'll read anything that's lying around. If he goes to a party, you may see him pick up a magazine and get totally absorbed in it. His wife often has to pull him out of the newspaper at home. He intends to come to the dinner table, but he *has* to finish that article.

Another weak point of our Thinker is that he can have a know-it-all attitude because he is so sure of his ideas. People claim he is impatient and doesn't listen to what they say. Ask him and he'll say they just haven't thought out their beliefs; that is, if he catches himself before he calls them idiots. In his worst moments his caustic tongue and contempt put others off.

David loves to argue. Sometimes it's passion for his ideas. Some Thinkers, however, argue for the pleasure of it.

Another thing about David — he feels the confusion of people around him. Don't make the mistake of believing that Thinkers don't feel anything. They feel ideas, and they feel people's confusion. Sometimes David thinks most people are crazy. Not in the sense of needing to be put in an institution — they just need someone (like him if they would listen) to sit them down and give them clarity.

The best version of someone like David is a true intellectual who wants to see reality. He has the ability to understand many things — academic subjects, the human body, religion, the stock market — and explain them to people in a way that makes sense.

The Feeler

Feelers love being with people. They're pros at relaxing and shooting the breeze. Their greatest spiritual pleasure is giving to others.

They love sharing experiences with friends and family.

They also love being out in nature. Beauty exhilarates them and lifts their soul. They love feeling the world around them, taking things in without the need to analyze them.

My friend Jeff is a great example of a Feeler. He has a real estate company in Miami. When I lived there in the late 1980s, I used to go to his house on the beach. I would bring a couple of books along to teach him; the purpose of our get-togethers was to learn something. Our appointment would be for 8 p.m., but we never got started before nine. First we had to have some hors d'oeurves. Then we had to go out on the patio, have a drink and watch the ocean for a half-hour. Finally, Jeff was ready to learn. I happen to be the Thinker type, so it took me a while to get used to his style.

Feelers have a pleasant, flowing lightness of character that makes them easy company. They enjoy life, are fun to be with and lift people through their natural buoyancy.

Feelers know how to make you sense they're with you and tuned into your emotions. Many of them go into helping professions. A Thinker and a Feeler would both be able to be psychologists, but they would tend to do it for different reasons. The Thinker wants to understand himself and others, and give people clarity. Feelers love helping people learn how to become happy.

When the Animal Soul controls Feelers, they can get caught up in hedonism because they feel physical pleasure so easily. A Thinker would have a hard time being a beach bum unless the beach was next door to a library. As for the Feeler — no problem, as long as there are lots of bodies around and the weather is good.

Thinkers go a little crazy from them, believing they lack intellectual depth. "Mush heads" is what they might call them. That's because Feelers are into relationships more than ideas. I'll give you a cute example. I once went to an evening class on counseling run by a brilliant Thinker. He was talking about how to develop empathy toward other people. At one point, a Feeler suggested that they shut off the lights, use candles and hold hands. "Are you kidding?" said the Thinker. He looked around the room. "Someone tell me he's kidding." The eyes of the Thinker flashed contempt at the poor Feeler. "I don't want to shock you, but the Sixties are dead," he snapped. So much for empathy from a wrathful Thinker.

Doers have a problem with Feelers, too. Doers tend to be disciplined and responsibility-oriented; Feelers are much less so, and can come off looking like babies who can't take pain.

Feelers have a trait that can either be a strength or weakness. Because they care about people so much, they hate confrontations and are always trying to make peace. But sometimes confrontations are necessary. Problems shouldn't be swept under the carpet in marriages, friendships or partnerships. If the Feeler knows how to disagree and handle the stress that comes with it, he is great at mediating. He can ask a neighbor to turn the music down without making it into a war. But if he hates confrontation, the problem can grow and grow.

If a Feeler gives rebuke, he has the ability to do it in a way that makes the other person know he cares. The Thinker can seem like he is calling the poor fellow an idiot. The Doer tends to drive over other people's feelings: "Just do what's right," he seems to say. "I don't care about your emotions."

My favorite type of Feeler is great at showing people the beauty of living and the blessings of existence. He is a warm, sympathetic listener who really cares about others. He's easygoing and fun to be with.

The Doer

Doers are action-oriented. They love implementing projects. They make great managers because of their work ethic and attention to detail.

Their central drive is to do the right thing. They are focused, determined and ready to act.

Their strength is in getting the job done. They will roll

up their sleeves and get to work when the other types are still keeping the couch warm.

Doers grind out work that drives Thinkers and Feelers crazy. Don't ever put a Thinker or Feeler in charge of logistics, such as managing a warehouse. The Thinkers will feel they are wasting their lives and the Feelers will keep looking for people to talk to.

Doers are great organizers of projects because they are so dependable and into doing tasks. Thinkers and Feelers would have a difficult, if not impossible time without them. Doers are able to implement the Thinker's ideas. They create the framework that enables Feelers to do their thing.

Doers make good businessmen because they aren't intimidated by a million mindless details. They do all the jobs Thinkers and Feelers hate to do.

If you are looking for a stereotype, Doers are the Boy Scouts of the world: self-sacrificing, hard workers.

Thinkers consider them robots who act without knowing why. Feelers consider them trucks that roll over other people's feelings while getting a job done.

Doers often love tasks even when the work is mundane. Thinkers *hate* tasks because they feel they are wasting their time. Feelers can get into projects if they enjoy the people they're working with; the task itself isn't as important.

The Animal Soul can take the strengths of the Doer and turn them against him. They can become obsessed with accomplishment and success. Doers often become competitive to prove their self worth. They need accomplishment and become fidgety and anxious when they are not in action. This can bring on guilt and push them to run around and do things compulsively.

One woman told me that she dreads waking up in the middle of the night, because she feels the need to drag herself out of bed and dust the furniture in her house. She feels she must be doing something constructive every minute, otherwise she is wasting time.

When a Doer is operating at top form, he or she is superb at getting a job done. It could be running a house, a project or a business – tasks are completed smoothly and on schedule.

The following chart summarizes the ideal behavior of the Thinker, Feeler and Doer:

The next chart summarizes potentially bad habits of the Thinker, Feeler and Doer:

Strengths of the Three Types

	Thinker	*Feeler*	*Doer*
Life Drive	Truth	Loves making others happy	Doing the right thing; getting the job done
Orientation	Ideas	People	Action; tasks
Description	Absorbed in figuring out the meaning of life	Loves people	Great at running projects, businesses and organizations
	Excited by ideas	Loves being with people	Gets things accomplished
	Driven to attain self-awareness	Loves to shoot the breeze	Great organizer
	Wants systematic understanding of life	Light, pleasant, flowing	Can grind out work
	Needs to know why	Enjoys life	Tough, takes pain
	Always analyzing himself, others and concepts	Gives off warmth	Reliable, dependable
	Constantly tries to improve his ideas	Shows people the beauty of living and the blessings of life	Self-sacrificing
	Wants to know how things work	Into nature, beauty	Boy Scout-type
		Optimistic, positive emotions	

Weaknesses of the Three Types

Thinker	Feeler	Doer
Easily distracted	Uncurbed desire	Gets down on himself, thinking he's not doing enough
Doesn't listen	Irresponsible	Obsessed with success
Know-it-all attitude	Happiness means escape	Fidgety, anxious, nervous
Sharp tongue	Low threshold for pain	Rolls over people when getting something done
Gets thrown off by confusion when it's around	Floater without clear goals	Highly competitive
Lack of clarity causes depression	Lazy, hangs around doing nothing	Obsessively runs around doing things
Day dreams; lost in ideas		
Plays devil's advocate		
Will read anything that's around		

Talking to the Three Types

We have all three types within us. We're all capable of caring about ideas and people, and making the trains run on time. Most of us, however, are inclined by nature to one of the three. This can cause a lot of communication difficulties, and even intolerance, between the Thinker, Feeler and Doer.

The Thinker, Feeler and Doer have very different motivations for their choices.

For example, let's say an old lady wants to cross the street. A Thinker will help her because it is the *sane* thing to do. The world shouldn't be a crazy jungle where all that counts is survival of the fittest.

The Feeler helps her because he *cares* about her and experiences her distress.

The Doer helps because it is the *right* thing to do. He may have no emotions toward her personally; he just wants to do a good deed.

Sometimes our choices combine elements of all three types.

If you want to convince someone to do something, whether it's a spouse, friend or customer, it's very helpful to figure out which type you're dealing with.

Let's say you'd like your friend to read this book so he can learn more about the soul. If he is a Thinker, tell him he'll get a lot of intellectual clarity from it. If he is a Feeler, talk about how it will improve his relationships and help him appreciate people more. If he is a Doer, tell him it will help him accomplish more and become a better human being.

How about if you are selling vacuum cleaners? Explain to the Thinker how the appliance works. Talk about what amazing modern features it has and why they have been added.

For the Feeler, point out that he or she will stay calm when the kids make a mess, because it's so easy to clean with the "miracle machine." The house will be more peaceful.

For the Doer, emphasize the efficiency. He or she will have more time to do other things.

And if you aren't sure which kind of person you have in front of you, get all three approaches in there.

Harmonizing the Types within Oneself

Ideally, the ten fundamental Forces (Crown, Wisdom, etc.) and the three types that descend from them (Thinker, Feeler, Doer) should all operate in harmony. The Talmud says:

> **"The world stands on three things: Torah, service and acts of lovingkindness."**

Yehuda Loeve (1526–1609), known as the Maharal of Prague, was a Kabbalist who wrote a lengthy explanation of this statement.* He clarified that "Torah" here refers to spiritual wisdom. "Service" is the drive to do the right thing, to be a good person. "Lovingkindness" is the ideal way to relate to other people.

In other words, we're talking about the Thinker, Doer and Feeler. (The order of the last two is reversed in the quotation.)

---

*The Maharal was famous as a saint and miracle worker. His reputation lasted for centuries. In 1917, the municipal government of Prague erected a statue of him in front of the city hall, where it stands to this day.

What does the Talmud mean when it says the world *stands* on these three qualities?

The least number of legs a chair can have without falling is three (unless it is cemented to the floor, of course). I've even seen some three-wheeled cars. The Talmud is telling us that if the world is lacking even one of these factors, it will topple from instability.

This is true of a country, also. Let's say the country is full of people who have a drive for spiritual enlightenment. That's all well and fine, but if it isn't joined with a compassion for others, the streets will be filled with hungry, homeless people.

Or what if the country is great on compassion, but helpless when it comes to implementation? People will care about each other, but the economy will be in shambles.

Or what if it scores high on action, but low on Thinkers? The country will lose its compass as to where it is heading, both in values and economic planning.

So it is clear that all three are needed.

A human being is also a world. Each one of us must be balanced in all three areas, even if by nature we are especially good at one.

Let me give an example of how this applies in parenting. If the parent has wisdom in knowing how to raise a child but doesn't convey love and support, the child probably won't listen.

If the parent feels and shows love but doesn't have wisdom, he won't teach clear values. He'll find it hard to say "no" because he can't stand hurting his child.

And if the parent is efficient at running the home and disciplining the child — a great Doer in this area — but poor at explaining decisions or showing love, the likelihood of failure is again great.

The best combination is wisdom, love and implementation. It's not a pie-in-the-sky ideal, but a necessity: "The world stands on three things," says the Talmud. Kick one leg away and the chair topples.

The principle also operates when it comes to running a business. If you have great ideas but lousy interpersonal skills, your staff will be morose. Also, you probably won't do well at sales without the warm, personal touch of a Feeler.

If you have great interpersonal skills and confused ideas, you'll also have difficulties. I know of a man who tried to build a factory on the honor system. The owner was a classic Feeler — a genuinely nice guy who cared a lot about his workers, but was naïve. He would often join them on the factory floor and have a beer. Enforcement was lax when they showed up late or left early. When an employee needed a loan, he gave it.

This poor fellow almost went out of business. Now he is bitter. He says everyone took advantage of him, so he was forced to institute tough rules. Everyone punches a time clock. He is inaccessible to his workers. If there are drug problems or fights, they are fired immediately. The workers are bitter, too.

What happens if you have great ideas and know when and how to empathize with workers and customers — but you lack implementation skills?

"You're a nice guy with a lot of clarity," clients will say. "So how come you're two days late with every delivery?" Try to sell pizzas with an apology. The competition will blow you out of business.

Get the point?

We should develop all three types within us, or at least surround ourselves with people who complement our weaknesses.

The fourth soul has within it the potential power of the Thinker, Feeler and Doer. By the time its powers filter down to the lowest soul, however, the physical body exerts its influence and weakens the impact. Even the second soul, the Spirit, specializes in only one of the three types.

Is there a way to get the most out of the powers rooted in fourth soul? The answer to this is yes!

To do so, each person must discover his own unique mission – a mission whose general outlines rest in the soul even before we are born. That is partially why people, such as the woman from Los Angeles who we met at the beginning of this chapter, are so interested in their roots. They are searching for a clue as to their identity. Isn't part of our identity what we are meant to accomplish in this world?

How do we discover our purpose in this world and tap into all the different powers of the fourth soul? We will turn our attention to this great topic in the next chapter.

CHAPTER 14

WRITING YOUR MISSION STATEMENT

> If you would hit the mark, you must aim a little above it; every arrow that flies feels the attraction of earth.
> *Henry Wadsworth Longfellow, Elegiac Verse*

I HAVE A FRIEND NAMED ELLIOTT WHO GAVE $5 million to a university so that his name would be put on a building.

"You know why I did it?" We were talking recently in his living room. He showed me a picture of a large, pink-stoned edifice. Sure enough, his name was on it. "That building will last for a long time. My grandchildren and even their kids after them will be able to point to it and say, 'My old man donated the money for that place.'"

"Elliott, you are a really generous guy," I said. But I wondered for a moment — what is he really after? If Elliott had said that his purpose for the donation was to further education, he surely would be attaining his goal.

If he wants to be remembered by future generations — I doubt any one will care in a hundred years, if even that. Is he looking for eternity? Approval?

The reason for asking such questions is not to take the wind out of good deeds; it's to make sure that we are clear in our *mission statement*. A mission statement describes what an individual or organization stands for and hopes to achieve.

Every one of us should have a mission statement, preferably written on a piece of paper so that we can look at it when we need to.

Companies have mission statements. For a supermarket, it may be "We want to provide the most convenient grocery shopping at the lowest prices in the city."

Sometimes a business loses sight of its mission statement and gets into trouble. I have a friend who was a Vice President at International Telephone and Telegraph during the 1980s, when the company was buying up everything in sight.

"IT&T is heading for trouble," he confided in me at that time. "It doesn't stand for anything anymore except making money. A business can't just be about making money. It has to unite behind some philosophy, like 'Our goal is to provide the best telephone service on the planet.'

"IT&T buys businesses that have no relationship to one another. When we put all the managers of the different subsidiaries around a table, they have nothing to talk about. As far as I can see, money alone won't hold us together."

IT&T ended up selling off some of these companies because they became time-consuming distractions.

This is also true for every one of us. We should all have

some kind of mission statement that describes our most important dream in life. Then we should marshal our resources in that direction.

I recently met a real estate developer from Turkey. I asked him what his life's goal was. "You can't imagine the feeling I get when I see one of my housing projects go up. I feel like I'm putting shelters over the heads of thousands of people." Part of his goal was making money, of course. But that alone wouldn't have done it for him. In terms of his mission statement, he put it this way: "I want to build neighborhoods that house thousands of people, provide them with a good lifestyle, and make very good money in the process."

For another person, it could be to become a great math teacher. If pressed on why, the person might say, "I want to help kids develop their talents and self-confidence. Math provides me with a way to do this." Once he awakens to the real drive under it all — helping kids — he will probably look for additional ways to accomplish his goal, including with his own children.

Having a mission statement doesn't mean that you become possessed by one fixed idea. You can put up good houses and go to jazz concerts, too.

Nor does it mean that your statement is engraved on stone. You can always write a new one if you outgrow the old dream.

It *does* mean you have purpose and clear direction in your life.

Here's the bottom line in the most ideal mission statement: if pursued, it should give you a payback now — and for eternity.

The Soul Is Eternal

Let's talk about why our mission statement should take eternity into account.

Kabbala teaches us that the soul lives forever. Imagine how much happier people would be if they were confident about this. Human beings expend incredible amounts of effort trying to ensure that they continue to exist in one way or another. Some people want to leave a monument to their memory. My friend who gave $5 million to get his name on a building is an example.

Artists want their paintings hanging in museums. Many authors want to write a classic. This too is the hope for eternity. But does it really make a difference if a thought of him remains in someone's mind, when the painter or author himself turns to dust? This is like scratching your name on the wall of a hotel room, and thinking you've left your mark on history because some occupant will see it in five years. *But you're gone!*

It is of course wonderful to give a meaningful gift to the world. But I want to know that I continue to exist, not just the fruits of my labor.

Some people hope to continue to exist by having children and grandchildren. Kids are great. I love my children. But I also have a life of my own. It's bad enough to live through your children in this world, but to hope to do it permanently is really futile.

The only *real* eternity is for the soul to exist forever, with its memory and accomplishments intact. Kabbala teaches that this is exactly what happens. What we do on Earth brings out the latent dynamism of the fourth soul, and gives it powers that it will carry forever. That's why it's so important to have a mission statement; otherwise, we risk losing focus and wasting our potential.

A Mansion in Eternity

A perfectly tailored mission statement should reflect the root of our talents, which is in the fourth soul.

Kabbala teaches that before we come into our Earthly body, each of us is shown his potential accomplishments and place in the afterlife, according to the root of his soul.

Imagine you are shown a movie in which a real estate agent takes you to a gorgeous mansion in Beverly Hills. The grounds are expansive and the inside of the house is perfect for you.

You love the place. "How will I ever afford this?" you ask yourself.

You go back to your old house scratching your head, wondering what to do. Suddenly the phone rings and a friend is on the line with a business idea that will make you a fortune.

Who wouldn't be happy at such a turn of events?

That's what it's like for the soul before it enters the body. It is shown what its place can be in the afterlife. This is a billion times greater than that house in Beverly Hills!

The soul is also shown what its powers are and what it needs to do during its time on Earth in order to get the mansion afterwards. That's like the great business idea.

Kabbala teaches us that we get the mansion by discovering and living our mission statement. (We'll talk more about the "mansion" and the stages a person goes through after death when we get to the fifth soul.)

The ultimate root of our talents and mission is in the

fourth soul. When we truly use these talents, we actually increase the power and illumination of this fourth soul. This light then filters down to the three souls below it.

This light remains with us forever, even after the body drops off. The fourth soul is eternal, and brings the souls below it to eternity. (This resembles lifting one part of a necklace — all the other links are pulled along.)

We all make good and bad choices when we are in this world. The beautiful fact is this: the fourth soul is so lofty that it can't be destroyed by bad mistakes. Did you ever experience a time in life when many things seemed to be going wrong, yet you knew that deep inside you there was something that hadn't been ruined? This hidden pearl is the fourth soul and the other three connected to it. We can make a thousand silly decisions — the root of our talents and mission is always there, waiting to be drawn upon.

A few years ago, I was on a transatlantic flight and watched "McGuire," the film that created the popular expression, "Show me the money!"

Jerry McGuire is a fabulously successful sports agent living in the fast lane. He thinks he's achieving his dream — fame, money and women. His life crisis comes when one of his clients, a hockey player, gets badly smashed up in the rink. If he plays again it could be fatal, and he'll only listen to Jerry. Jerry can't tell him to quit. The money is too big.

Jerry finally realizes he's sold out to the dollar and remembers that other things count in life, too.

In the middle of the night he writes a new mission statement that talks about caring about the players and not just grabbing the pot of gold. His agency fires him when he sticks the mission statement in everyone's mailbox at work. But Jerry is a new man. He starts helping people again, turns a fading football star around and finds the girl who believes in him.

What's the point?

You've got to know your dream and live it. It will make your life unbelievably better *now*. You will feel fulfilled because you will be doing something meaningful, and not just working your head off for everyone else's dream.

If you are truly fortunate, you will create something that will bring in money and give you financial independence. Any good businessman will tell you that if you do something you have a passion for, your odds are infinitely greater to succeed. Even if your life dream doesn't make money and you have to get a different job, at least part of your day will be aimed at something immensely important to you.

Some people are afraid of writing out their mission statement. They fear that if they don't live it, they will feel like a failure for the rest of their life.

Why does it have to be all or nothing? Even if you only live 10% of your dream, it's a wonderful thing to do! It's not all or nothing — a mansion or you'll be out on the street.

A friend once said to me, "Ideals are like stars. We never totally reach them, but they help us navigate toward our destination."

Don't be afraid to go for your dreams. That would be like never playing baseball because you might not hit a home run every time you come to the plate. That's crazy. What about the fresh air and sunshine? The fun of playing on a team and meeting interesting people? Hitting singles, doubles and triples, and maybe even a few home runs? Batting .300 is considered excellent, though it means you failed seven out of ten times.

We accomplish in proportion to what we attempt. What a mission statement does is focus you on where you want to go. Furthermore, it's the greatest way to harness the major powers of the fourth soul, which contain the roots of thinking, feeling and doing.

Your unique mission statement is already sitting inside you, waiting to be discovered. How do you articulate it?

Everyone Has a Blessing

I have a game that I play with people in my seminars. After talking with someone for a minute (enough to give me a bit of a feel for their personality), I say, "I want to tell you what your blessing is."

The person naturally asks, "My what?"

"Your blessing. Do you know what a blessing is?"

"When good things happen to you, I guess."

"That's right," I answer. "When we say that someone is blessed, we mean life has given him many gifts. *It's also possible to bless someone.* You can actually give someone a blessing."

"I've heard of that. Don't religious leaders sometimes give blessings?"

"What do you think when you hear about that?"

"I think it's hocus pocus. I don't trust it. How can someone have the power to bless another person and cause good things to happen to him?"

"Well," I say, "I'm talking about a different type of

blessing. Every person has a unique potential in his soul. If he or she could reach that potential, it would be a source of far greater pleasure than just getting material things."

"I agree."

"The point of the blessing I want to give you, is to help you see your unique gifts. I want to lift you into a vision of your potential."

"You mean your blessing will show me who I could really be?"

"You've got it."

"Go ahead!"

One time, I was talking with a college student who said that he was bored by his classes. It was obvious that he was an idealist who wanted to help people. He was studying psychology and learning how different elements of personality work. He wasn't getting enough insight into values or spirituality, however, which is what he was really looking for.

So I gave him the following blessing: "May you gain the wisdom to show people how to be happy. May you find the way to bring them to God."

He almost jumped out of his seat. "I've been thinking about that a lot lately!" he exclaimed. "How did you know?"

Indeed, how *did* I know? It's not so mysterious — I've learned how to feel elements of the fourth soul that have filtered into someone's personality, often without him realizing it.

The college student was bored because his classes were not giving him the information he wanted. He wasn't getting anywhere in terms of his mission statement (which he hadn't yet clearly formulated). Does this mean he should quit college? Of course not. Most classes in university are not meant to teach what he was looking for. A degree, however, would be helpful to him in the future. It does mean that he should put aside part of his day to read books and meet people that can give him this kind of information. Then he should pick a career that would line up with his passions (psychologist, clergy, etc). If he can't get work in a career like this, he should get a different job and spend part of his day implementing his mission statement of helping other people spiritually.

A mission statement describes what we really want to do in life. It's imprinted in the fourth soul. I have a friend who has made millions of dollars in real estate. Several years ago, he was not a particularly happy man. "Dave," I told him, "you should fund a think tank that will work on solutions for peace in the hot spots of the world." That really was his drive — helping solve conflicts in a big way. He himself never could have done the academic research. But he is a fantastic businessman who loves making money and just needed to put some of it in a place that lined up with his mission statement, which was to help bring world peace.

If he hadn't made big money, he could have found another way to bring peace, like inviting people from different races together in his living room.

Think about one of your friends and try to imagine what he really wants to do underneath his daily whirlpool of activities. You'll surprise yourself at how good you can get at this game. And when you tell it to the person, you'll be amazed at how often his eyes light up. Even if you are wrong, the topic gets people to think about what they really want out of life.

Now take a look at yourself. If you had the means to accomplish anything you wanted, what would you do?

Some people say, "Lie on the beach in the Bahamas."

"Sounds nice for a few weeks," I tell them. "Believe me, you'd soon get bored."

"Are *you* ever wrong," each one says. "Just try me. I would love it!"

Okay, go do it. If that is your mission statement, try it out and see if it works.

If it does, fine and dandy. I wonder if it will. Did you ever hear about retirees who start going a little crazy? Golf may be nice for a while, but they soon start wanting to feel useful and productive, even at age seventy-five.

The fourth soul is always calling out to us from afar. "Bring forth my hidden light!" it cries out. "I want to accomplish things that are so beautiful!"

If we listen to the fourth soul and have the courage to live at least part of our dreams, we will begin our voyage to greatness.

Getting it on Paper

Try this exercise. On the following lines, write down your mission statement. Here is a good way to think of it: if nothing stood in your way, what would you really hope to accomplish during your lifetime?

_____

_____

_____

_____

If you knew you wouldn't be able to take anything from this world with you except what you accomplish in this mission statement, would you still be happy with what you wrote?

If you wrote, "Have a bank account with three million dollars in it," probably not. The fourth soul can never be satisfied with money alone, for what is money to it? How can it use it in the next world?

The fourth soul knows that money can be used in this world if it is for something meaningful. Therefore it isn't bad in itself. It's just that something else has to come with it if you want to be happy.

Your blessing should be your mission statement. If you're not satisfied with it, try again. If you are hitting a total block, ask several friends the following question: "What do you think is the greatest accomplishment I could attain, given who I truly am?" Hopefully the right friend will help you hit the mark.

I strongly urge you to write something down even if it is far from perfect. Look at it the next day. Are you comfortable with what you wrote?

If not, tinker with your statement again and again. Look at it a week later. When you finally have something you like, start "navigating" by it.

Relationships

Your mission statement will probably effect the kinds of friends you choose. How do we pick our friends? Often by chance. It might be a neighbor, or somebody we sat down next to in a class in college. It also might be someone we met at work.

One positive outcome of having a clear mission statement is that we start looking for people who will help us achieve our life goals. I'm not suggesting we should use people and that friends are merely rungs on our ladder to success. But it is natural to gravitate toward people who share similar interests and passions, even if their personality traits are very different.

The Talmud quotes a famous sage as saying, "I learned much wisdom from my teachers and even more from my friends."

A good friend acts as a sounding board for your dreams. Sometimes you even work together toward common life goals.

The same is true of choosing the right marriage partner. Nachum Braverman, a good friend of mine, wrote a book called "The Death of Cupid." He actually defines marriage. He puts it like this: "Marriage is the commitment a man and woman make to pursue their life goals together." These life goals should be embodied in your mission statement. If your mission is to become a violinist and turn people on to beauty, I hope you don't marry someone who hates music. You're going to be with a person who doesn't want to share an extremely important part of your life. He or she doesn't have to *become* a musician, but it is important to be with someone who cares about your goals (and vice versa).

I was recently at an airport lounge and struck up a conversation with a man who started telling me about the difficulties in his marriage. (Sometimes people open up to a stranger. I think they need to get things off their chest, and don't have a real friend they can trust.)

"My marriage is in trouble," he said sadly. "My wife

doesn't care about what's important to me in life. When-ever I try to tell her some of my dreams, she shuts off in-side."

"Well, what *are* your dreams?" I asked.

"Maybe you'll laugh at me," he said, sitting back in his chair. "I would like to take three months and go on a spiritual retreat somewhere. Financially I can pull it off. My wife just has no interest in it. I've been in business for twenty years and have neglected that part of my person-ality. Now I'd love a recharge."

"Have you told your wife that you're feeling spiritual exhaustion, that you want to get more meaning out of life?"

"She just doesn't relate to it," he said. "If she goes shop-ping and finds something new for her wardrobe, that's recharge enough for her."

"Do you have kids?"

"Yes, a boy and a girl."

"Here's an idea," I said. "Decide what kind of spir-itual retreat you would enjoy. Get a list of places, and pick one that is near good shopping and a camp for your kids. Instead of going for three months, tell your wife you would like to go for a week. If she agrees and has a good time when you go, next year she might try it for a longer pe-riod."

He really perked up. He opened his briefcase and pulled out a note pad.

"Sure," I said, "you'd be giving something to every-body. Build as a team. Then you might get exactly what you want."

"What do you mean?"

"If you want your wife to care about what's impor-tant to you, you have to care about what's important to her. Give her a chance."

His eyes lit up. "I think you've hit the target!"

He wanted to do the right thing. He was just going through a bit of a mid-life crisis and needed to take a break.

I gave him my phone number. He called back several weeks later full of enthusiasm. "It looks like it's going to be a road with a few bumps on it, but my wife likes the idea of taking off a few weeks and finding a place like you described. She's even willing to go to a few classes with me."

In choosing a marriage partner, you can see that it is critical to pick someone who sympathizes with your mission statement. And your future marriage partner should be the kind of person who helps you through adjustments in your goals along the way.

Putting it all together

Let's summarize what we have learned about the fourth soul.

It harbors the potential mission of each individual. It also contains the roots of spiritual powers that give a person the ability to think, feel and do. Most of us are good in one or two of these areas. To make full use of our potential in all three, we need powerful mission statements that motivate and focus us.

By being clear on our mission statement and putting it into practice, we will be able to harmonize and actualize the roots of the fourth soul and give it power that will last for eternity.

And if a person doesn't get his mission statement clear? He is like a carpenter who has the finest tools in the world, but doesn't know what he wants to build. He's not going to accomplish very much.

Now we have come to the last part of our journey. What happens to the soul after death? How should that affect us during this life? To answer these awesome questions we will now enter the realm of the fifth soul.

ULTIMATE ENLIGHTENMENT AND THE FIFTH SOUL

> The awakening in the morning
> is like the World to Come.
> *Chapters of Rebbi Eliezer 34*

ONE SNOWY AFTERNOON IN THE WINTER OF 1989, I went to Washington, D.C., to visit the president of a major university. (I would tell you his name, but I think he would be uncomfortable with this story.) I was living in nearby Potomac, Maryland, at the time.

The purpose of my visit was simple. I wanted him to spend an hour once a month studying one of the texts of Kabbala. A mutual friend had suggested the idea.

"Why do you want me to study?" he asked as I sat down in a comfortable armchair in his office.

His face was kind, scholarly — and extremely distracted. He looked as if he had five appointments waiting for him in other rooms.

"I have several excellent reasons," I said. "First of all, you'll love it and gain tremendously. But even more importantly, you are a role model for the whole university. If students know that you study sacred texts because you enjoy growing spiritually, it will be an incredible inspiration for them."

"You know, I think I would really enjoy something like that. It's a great idea. There's only one problem."

"What's that?" I asked.

"I don't have a minute of free time. I don't even have time for my own family. There are constantly crises in the university that I have to deal with."

As if to confirm what he was saying, the phone suddenly rang. He spoke quietly into the receiver for a moment, then hung up and looked at me.

"Do you know who that was?" he said.

"No, who?"

"Ex-President Reagan. He wanted advice about a book that someone's writing about him. You see what I mean? I want spirituality, I really do. But I don't have time!"

I was sad that such a fine person was treating himself so poorly. He walked with me out of his office and repeated in the outer reception room, "I know I should study with you, but I just can't do it!" As he finished the last word, a giant chunk of the ceiling fell down and missed his head by less than an inch. He looked at the pile of rubble on the floor and the little cloud of dust rising out of it and exclaimed, "I'm *still* not going to learn!" Then he turned, walked straight into his office and closed the door.

The two secretaries were wide-eyed with shock. "Has a piece of the ceiling ever fallen down before?" I asked.

"No!" they blurted out.

I went out to the street, marveling that someone could get such a clear message and push it away.

I know that people want transcendent experiences. I feel their genuine yearning to get closer to God, the Creator, cosmic consciousness or whatever word you feel comfortable with.

Yet many people are uneasy, even scared. They feel as if they are in danger if they get too close. A nice walk in the woods is one thing. Unity with Oneness is like entering a hole in space and disappearing into the unknown.

Don't be afraid of closeness to the source of all love and creation! *Within us we truly want a relationship with God.* The Kabbalists tell us that every human being has a spot of inner discomfort, no matter how happy he or she is. That discomfort is a haunting inner awareness of our own vulnerability. We sense that we are somehow missing an overpowering beauty and calm.

Ultimately, money won't give it to us. Even wonderful relationships won't fully give it to us. It can only come from unity with our Creator.

The fifth soul gives us this unity.

The Fifth Soul

The fifth soul, like the fourth, exists outside of the physical body. It's called the *Yechida*, which means "Unique Essence." The *Yechida* is so pure that it exists on a level of intense closeness with the Source of all creation.

There is no experience more pleasurable than merging the five souls into one, and basking in the glow of unity with God. Think of the greatest moments of happiness in your life, and you will have a hint of the rapture involved. Your child was born; you watched the sun go down over the mountains; you saved someone's life — these moments lift a human being toward the transcendental. The spirituality is so powerful, we can almost touch it. Yet a few minutes later...we are subject to forgetfulness.

After death, all of the other souls unite with the fifth soul. We will experience a closeness to the Creator that will be Eternal.

We desire to live with all five levels of soul united on Earth right now, but the Animal Soul prevents us.

All of us are aware of the Animal Soul while we are alive. This is the force that animates us in our everyday affairs. Lofty spiritual experiences that come from connection to higher levels of the soul, however, don't happen as often. Absolute unity with God occurs even less.

Most people have no revelation at all of the *Yechida* — the fifth soul — during life on Earth, because it doesn't reside in the body. Only after death do they experience it, when the four souls and the fifth soul reunite and they feel intense unity with God.

This is the perfect time to discuss what happens after death.

Exiting the Body

The Zohar talks about what the soul undergoes when it first exits the physical body. I find it fascinating that the descriptions parallel those stated by hundreds of people who have experienced "clinical death." A number of doctors and researchers have written extensively about this subject in recent years.

Dr. Raymond Moody's book, "Life after Life," created something of a sensation when it first came out. He writes of cases in which, at the point of greatest physical stress, a patient hears himself pronounced dead. Then he begins to hear a loud noise and feels himself rushing through a long tunnel. Suddenly, he is outside of his body and looking at it from a distance. He is in a state of emotional upheaval. He sees the spirit of relatives and friends who have died. A loving spirit of light appears that he has never before experienced. He is asked questions to make him evaluate his life, the major events of which flash before him. Then he finds himself coming toward some type of border, which seems to designate the limit between the physical world and the afterlife. He is overwhelmed by powerful feelings of happiness, love and peace.

That's when the patient hears a voice telling him that he has to return to his body and to life in our world, which he does.

And how do the Kabbalists describe what happens to the soul after death?

For people who have led truly spiritual lives, the moment of death is not terrible. The Talmud compares it to "pulling a hair out of milk." This is because the soul doesn't fight its departure when the fitting moment comes.

People who have been ruled by the Animal Soul, however, leave this world with pain and fear. The Talmud says that their souls depart "like a knotted rope that can only be pulled out of the ship's mast with great effort." Their soul has become so interconnected to the body that it desperately resists separation from it.

In either case, as death comes, the soul begins to disengage from the body. The Zohar (the central text of Kabbala) says:

... A noise begins which only the dying person can hear...A new spirit enters into him from above, through which he sees things he could not see before. (Vayechi 167)

The Animal Soul is exposed to a powerful radiance coming from God. The Zohar says:

A human being doesn't die until he sees the Divine light, toward which his Animal Soul goes out in great yearning. (Emor 5)

Thus the soul departs from the body and enters the Spiritual World. The Divine light coaxes out even those who are very reluctant to depart.

Possibly this Divine light is the "Being of light radiating love and warmth" experienced by Dr. Moody's patients. Now we understand why, once out, they don't desire to return to their bodies.

The Zohar says that a person's whole life passes before him. He sees the choices he made and understands the tests he went through. Then he meets departed relatives and friends.

The soul continues to be aware of what is happening on Earth. The Zohar says that for the first seven days after death the soul travels from the grave to the house, back to the grave and to the house again, mourning for the body. For twelve months, it intermittently moves back and forth from its spiritual abode to Earth.

Then it remains in its place in the next world.

The Next World

The realm the soul inhabits after death is so abstract to people that they don't know how to imagine it. What happens there anyway? Are airy souls floating around without anything interesting to do? No food, no drinks, no sex, no sports — what do they do all day?

Mark Twain was so put off by the thought of a boring eternity that he quipped, "Heaven for climate and Hell for company."

Well, is the resting place of the soul pleasurable and interesting or not?

According to Kabbala, there are two possible places the soul can go after death. One is called *Gehenom* (there is really no word to translate it); and the other is called *Olam Haba*, or "the World to Come."

It may not be the most elegant comparison, but *Gehenom* performs the task of a powerful washing machine. Some clothes are moderately dirty and don't require heavy cleaning. Other clothing has gotten grimed up pretty well and requires a powerful cleansing cycle. The purpose of *Gehenom* is to purge the soul of defects it acquired from destructive choices made while in the physical world. This is the soul's grime. These defects are painful and shameful to the soul. The person goes through embarrassment and distance from the Divine light. The painful realizations purify the soul and open it to receiving intense, spiritual pleasure.

According to Kabbala, the soul remains in *Gehenom* no longer than one year. Then it moves into the World to Come, which is a paradise of spiritual illumination.

What does the soul do in the World to Come? The Talmud says people have no rest in the next world, for they go from group to group. What does this mean? The Kabbalists say they meet one assembly of wise people after another, and continue to grow and flourish.

What do they talk about with these people? All of the

things that they experienced in their journey through the physical world will be explained to them on an extraordinarily deeper level.

Kabbala also says that people sit with crowns on their heads and bask in the splendor of the Divine Presence. This is pretty much the same idea. It doesn't mean they literally have crowns or heads, because these are physical things that only exist on Earth. What it does mean, is that they have the pleasure of being in the presence of ultimate beauty and meaning. They understand their lives and add to the wisdom they gained in the physical world.

But there are limitations to the pleasures of the World to Come. There are no trees, mountains and sunsets, or the other physical things that give us hints and inspire us to think for ourselves. I said in an earlier chapter that the soul has all potential wisdom. When we enter the physical world, we begin to make choices that illuminate or darken this potential wisdom. Whatever is not retrieved and understood on Earth, however, is lost.

In the next world we experience spirituality through the wisdom that we attained, but the abstractions remain abstract. They cannot be understood anymore.

We need the experiences that come with having a body to awaken the knowledge of the soul. There is no body in Heaven. We will be deepening the concepts we already learned, but not breaking into new turf.

Don't be discouraged, though, for the journeys of the soul are not yet finished. We have more opportunities to accomplish greatness. Reincarnation is one of them.

Reincarnation

Even after the soul has reached the spiritual world it can sometimes reincarnate back into the physical world. The same soul can inhabit a succession of bodies. It is given a chance to fix damage done in previous lives and achieve a higher and higher degree of perfection. Each of these return trips is called a *gilgul*.

A reincarnation occurs because a soul in the first body wasn't able to complete its mission; therefore, it is born again.

This is not negative. It's not that the soul is trapped in a terrible cycle of rebirth until it can find release. Instead, think of it as a gift: reincarnation provides human beings with another opportunity to achieve their greatest dreams.

The Final Destination

There is one final journey remaining for all human beings.

Before learning about this period of time, I want to ask a question: "What exactly *is* a human being?"

Is a human being the soul with a body, or the soul by itself without a body? If you believe the latter, you may fall into the dangerous trap of thinking that the body is really a kind of prison. Death then becomes a release, enabling the soul to attain great happiness in Heaven because it escapes the physical world like a bird escaping its cage.

It is very dangerous to believe that the soul is the real "me" imprisoned in the physical world. This idea causes many people to think that the more they weaken and humiliate their body, the more they honor their soul. They become ascetics who deprive themselves of all the pleasures of life. They stay away from good food and think that sex should be severely reduced, or even totally avoided because it is somehow dirty. If they become extreme, they scourge and punish their body, thinking that this will make the spiritual side more powerful.

The soul should rule the body like a rider atop a horse. It shouldn't annihilate it!

The thought of only being among ascetics who detest the physical world made Twain quip, "Heaven for climate and Hell for company." According to Kabbala, he was misinformed: the soul world is filled with people who enjoyed their lives. We can take pleasure safely if we use the principles discussed in this book and don't let the body smother our spirituality.

Kabbala believes that a human being is a soul and a body together, not a soul trapped in a prison. The body isn't a human being. The soul isn't a human being. *Both of them together are.*

Without both, you and I are not fully human.

Why? The reason is that we must have freedom to choose. Without the ability to choose, to affect things, to make a difference – human beings never attain true happiness. We merely exist. The physical world is the place that we make a difference, by taking what is imperfect and improving it. We, of course, learn and grow in the process.

The reason for death is that the body attains such power over the soul, that the two must be separated. The soul then realizes that it lost control, made mistakes and diminished its power while living on Earth.

At the moment of death, the soul clearly sees this. It

enters the spirit world and experiences sublime delight (with a possible "cleansing" delay of up to one year, as I said earlier in this chapter). It shines with a radiance that befits it as a result of the good choices it made while on Earth. Thus, it is able to regain power that it might have lost while being associated with the physical world.

The ultimate goal of the soul, however, is not simply to exist in a relaxed state, even a very pleasurable one. Human beings love choosing and growing. The place for such growth is the physical world. Therefore, the soul will ultimately be brought back to Earth. This true ultimate period of meaning for the soul is called "Resurrection of the Dead." It is an epoch when all souls will be taken out of the soul world and permanently reunited with bodies.

When this happens, we will be fully human again with feelings, choices and the ability to relate to one another. We will enjoy existence with both body and soul. The soul will have so much power after it is resurrected, that it will no longer be bound or restricted, and will enter the body with immense brilliance and strength. Even the Animal Soul will be illuminated. The body will then experience a great enlightenment. The new, complete man will be able to elevate himself forever in the physical world.

What will it be like to walk the planet when humanity will be resurrected this way?

In its earlier appearance on Earth (or appearances, if it was reincarnated), the soul already had a great amount of natural perfection. Mistaken choices held it back, however, and prevented it from functioning freely.

When the soul recombines with a body after the Resurrection, it will no longer be as a novice making wrong choices. Instead, it will shine forth and illuminate the body to an extraordinary degree.

This doesn't mean that resurrected man won't be able to keep growing as a person and elevating himself. There is an endless amount of wisdom to be learned from the leaf of a tree or the poetry of a soaring bird. Everything in the world was created through a combination of Kabbalistic Forces and can be studied almost infinitely, just as the Creation can yield continuous insights to a scientist.

The body, however, will no longer be able to dominate. In the first period after Resurrection, a person will feel a bit of heaviness because the soul at this stage doesn't have the strength to expand in all its power. As time goes on, the five parts of the soul will be thoroughly united with the body, so that a person will experience the most exalted state possible.

There will no longer be war or hatred. The physical world that had been so sullied, worn and polluted will yield immense spirituality. The world will seem like a house whose curtains have been lifted and windows thrown open.

This has been the goal of all of history — the struggle to bring the physical world to perfection. There has always been a clash between light and darkness within the human species. Sometimes darkness prevailed until it seemed as if humanity would destroy itself; at other times, human beings managed to work together, spreading beauty and wisdom.

The same is true of individuals. Each of us begins as a baby whose Animal Soul holds the stage. As we mature, we strain toward the enlightenment that our higher souls so passionately desire. In adult life, sometimes the Animal Soul dominates and other times the higher souls rule.

After the Resurrection, the physical world and its inhabitants will cross a threshold of perfection, never to turn back.

Imagine yourself unhindered by worry or fear, able to penetrate the innermost mysteries of existence. You will be able to command the powers of nature and experience the presence of the Creator. The pleasure of growth and accomplishment will be eternal.

You will have mastered the powers of the soul!

\\\\\\\\\\\\\\\\\\\\\\\\\\\\\\\\

This, then, brings us to the end of the journey we have taken together.

You have probably seen hundreds of people in the past week, in the streets and buildings of your city or even on television. The pressures and details of daily existence often distract them, but they want the same thing as you and I: to discover their inner powers, to accomplish meaningful goals and to live life to the fullest.

The principles in *Powers of the Soul* help achieve this. Thank you for giving me the opportunity to share this knowledge with you.

Epilogue

A few years ago, I was teaching weekly evening classes on Kabbala. At the end of one session, I gave the students an exercise: take a fifteen-minute walk in a pleasant place and try to feel God's presence.

I promised to phone each of them as a reminder during the week. I managed to reach everyone but a young lawyer named Susan, who I didn't talk to until the day of the class.

"Susan," I said. "I'm calling to remind you about last week's exercise. Did you do it?"

"Oh, Rabbi, I've been so busy! But I promise to focus on it before class tonight."

The students gathered in my living room that evening. Everyone was there except Susan. I had given up on her when there was a knock at the door. She entered looking pale and unsettled.

The students had already described their experiences. When she sat down I asked, "Susan, did you have a chance to do it?"

"Well," she said, "I was very tired when I finished work this evening. I started to drive to the class and focus on what you taught us, but my head was blank. I was too exhausted. So I decided to stop at a donut shop and order a cup of coffee.

"As I was sitting there I noticed an advertisement for one of those instant-lottery tickets. I thought to myself,

'Sometimes I'm not even sure if I have a soul, or if there is a God or any meaning to life at all. Here's a chance to find out! I have never won anything in my life. If I buy one of these tickets right now and win, then I am being sent a clear message.'

"I bought a ticket and rubbed it with a coin to reveal the hidden numbers. Let me ask you Rabbi, what do you think happened?"

All the students leaned forward with anticipation.

Susan stood up, opened her purse and handed me $300. "Please give it to charity," she said.

She left at the end of class and, unfortunately, soon became overwhelmed with career pressures. Her personal life went on the back burner. For weeks I called to invite her back. Finally after six months she returned.

To live like a soul takes determination. Sometimes it also requires a caring friend or teacher who makes sure that we don't forget who we are.

Let me tell you one final story. It happened to me a few nights ago. I was watching my two-year-old son Eli chasing a red balloon around the living room. Every time he grabbed the balloon, it popped out of his hands.

Another one of my sons, Aaron (who is a teenager), couldn't stop laughing. "He's so silly, Dad. Why doesn't he just give up?"

"We're all chasing something, Aaron. If it's important enough, we *shouldn't* give up. If he's running after balloons when he's your age, we'll have a problem on our hands. It's our job to teach him to go after great things."

"I get it, Dad. I guess I should be thinking about what I run after."

Bull's-eye.

My little Eli feels safe and happy. All of life is his playground and he's grasping at it with gusto.

The same is true for us. And we have the powers of the soul to help us achieve our goals.

ACKNOWLEDGMENTS

In 1972, I was a journalist for a newspaper in Detroit. One morning we were understaffed. I finished my article and rushed it to press without it being edited. A bad mistake! I left out a piece of information that made the story incomprehensible.

I learned an important lesson: make sure other people read your manuscript before it goes to print!

I received excellent advice and encouragement on *Powers of the Soul* from many wonderful people. Rena Berger, Robin Berman, Adam Winston, Noah Wyle, Zelig Pliskin, Shaul Rosenblatt and Sammy Kassin deserve special mention.

Charlie and Nancy Ganz encouraged me to write this book long before the first words appeared on a page.

I would also like to thank Dr. Robert and Elyse Furlong, and Bill and Phyllis Marcus for their strong support.

Rabbi Noah Weinberg will recognize his influence. I am grateful to him for many years of imparted wisdom.

Peter Berger also deserves special mention. He prodded me a thousand times, sometimes lugging a procrastinating author and his word processor out to a restaurant.

My wife, Sheryl, helped edit the manuscript and was the sounding board along the way. Much more importantly, her love has been the raft that has navigated every river.

My brother-in-law, Irwin Katsof, provided inspiration as he labored at his own book, *Powerful Prayers*. So did Rabbi Nachum Braverman, who recently published *The Death of Cupid*.

ABOUT THE AUTHOR

Rabbi Tom Meyer gives lectures worldwide on Judaism and mysticism. He has had a diversified career: he was a journalist for the Detroit News and flew into Israel during the 1973 war. His experiences in Jerusalem intrigued him, and he began studying Talmud and eventually Kabbala. He quit his job as a reporter and, after nine years of study, received rabbinical ordination.

He didn't feel he had the temperament to become a congregational rabbi. Instead, he opened a school in Washington, D.C., where he taught courses using the classical texts of Judaism. He also taught ethics classes on Capitol Hill.

Rabbi Meyer has returned to Jerusalem, where he currently lives with his wife and children.

To order more copies of **Powers of the Soul**, please send $14.00 US, plus $2.50 to cover postage and handling. Send check or money order, no cash or C.O.D.'s, please.

Name _____

Address _____

City/State/Zip _____

Send order to: Upward Bound Books
                  P.O. Box 200
                  Bergenfield, New Jersey 07621

In Israel: Upward Bound Books
                  26/1 Nachal Refayim
                  Beit Shemesh 97200

Allow four weeks for delivery. Prices and availability subject to change without notice.